CALIFORNIA
Brandy Cuisine

CALIFORNIA
Brandy Cuisine

Celebrating 200 Years of California Brandy

by

Malcolm Hébert

PUBLISHED BY THE WINE APPRECIATION GUILD

Other books published by The Wine Appreciation Guild:

THE CHAMPAGNE COOKBOOK
EPICUREAN RECIPES OF CALIFORNIA WINEMAKERS
GOURMET WINE COOKING THE EASY WAY
FAVORITE RECIPES OF CALIFORNIA WINEMAKERS
DINNER MENUS WITH WINE
EASY RECIPES OF CALIFORNIA WINEMAKERS
THE POCKET ENCYCLOPEDIA OF CALIFORNIA WINE
IN CELEBRATION OF WINE AND LIFE
WINE CELLAR RECORD BOOK
CORKSCREWS: Keys to Hidden Pleasures
THE CALIFORNIA WINE DRINK BOOK
THE CALIFORNIA BRANDY DRINK BOOK
NEW ADVENTURES IN WINE COOKERY
WINE IN EVERYDAY COOKING
THE WINE LOVERS' COOKBOOK

THE VINTAGE IMAGE SERIES:

THE NAPA VALLEY TOUR BOOK
THE NAPA VALLEY WINE BOOK
THE SONOMA MENDOCINO TOUR BOOK
THE SONOMA MENDOCINO WINE BOOK
THE CENTRAL COAST TOUR BOOK
THE CENTRAL COAST WINE BOOK

Published by:

The Wine Appreciation Guild
1377 Ninth Avenue
San Francisco, CA 94122
(415) 566-3532
(415) 957-1377

In cooperation with:

California Brandy Advisory Board

Library of Congress Catalog Number: 83-051171
ISBN: 0-932664-46-6
Printed in the United States of America
Book Design: Ronna Nelson
Editor: Donna Bottrell
Asst. Editors: Susan Lang, Ray Simmons, Larry Williams
Historical Consultant: Charles L. Sullivan

Table of Contents

Foreword

Happy 200th birthday, California brandy

The following pages are meant to inspire food for the body, not food for thought and debate among history scholars. Nonetheless, it seems worthwhile to establish the rationale for celebrating the 200th anniversary of California brandy in 1984.

There is no specific, verifiable, recorded date for the very first brandy distilled in the part of the world we now call the State of California. Nor is there a need for such documentation. While historians might quibble over specific dates and place the introduction of brandy to California earlier or later than 1784, there are some things few serious researchers would debate.

First, the antiquity of brandy in California is a clearly indisputable historic fact. The Spaniards brought winegrowing culture with them as they moved up the west coast of Mexico in the 16th and 17th centuries. They planted grapes, made wine and distilled it into brandy. They carried their mission system across the Gulf of California into Baja, or Lower California, during the 17th century.

Author-historian Charles L. Sullivan states, "It is generally accepted, (among historical scholars), that Father Juan Ugarte was Lower California's first vineyardist, at Mission San Francisco Xavier in 1697. By 1768, the year before the establishment of the San Diego mission, there were at least five Lower California missions with vineyards producing wine and brandy."

Major historians agree there was a steady flow of brandy from Lower to Upper California for the first 30 to 40 years after new missions were established in what we now call California, U.S.A. Hubert Howe Bancroft in his voluminous *History of California,* published in San Francisco in 1886, cites the manifest of the ship *San Carlos* on its first expedition to San Diego in 1769. On board were "5 jars of brandy" and "6 jars of Cal. wine." Bancroft also makes specific reference to the ship *Favorita,* which probably carried brandy to the southern missions of Upper California in 1784.

The question of just when the Upper California missions began producing their own wine and brandy is a controversial one. Nevertheless Sullivan says there has been ample scholarly work done since World War II on this question and it has been consistent, logical and based on solid research.

The concensus is, according to Sullivan, that no wines were produced, (and therefore no brandies), from the vines or grape cuttings brought to Mission San Diego in 1769. His "educated guess" is that the first wine produced in Upper California "could have been as early as 1782, but might have been 1783."

Research by Edith B. Webb in her *Indian Life at the Old Missions,* (Los Angeles, 1952) led wine writer Roy Brady to nominate Padre Pablo Mugartegui of Mission San Juan Capistrano as California's first wine-maker in 1782. Brady's well reasoned analysis, "The Swallow that Came from Capistrano," (*New West,* September 24, 1979) has been recently accepted by Ruth Teiser and Catherine Harroun in their *Winemaking in California,* (New York, 1983).

While agreeing the first California wine was produced at San Juan Capistrano, the vintage year is set as 1784 by Jacob N. Bowman in "The Vineyards in Provincial California," *Wine Review,* April-July 1943, and by Herbert B. Leggett in "Early History of Wine Production in California," masters thesis, History Department, University of California, Berkeley, April 2, 1939. Vincent Caruso also accepted the 1784 date in his University of California doctoral dissertation in 1950 and in his later published work, *The California Wine Industry, 1830-1895,* (Berkeley, 1951).

Sullivan concludes the date of the first California wine vintage can be selected from 1782, 1783 or 1784 since each of these dates depends on educated guesses, based on the historical data available.

Sadly none of the historians has offered positive proof of brandy being distilled in Upper California before 1800. To fill in this gap in historical data, I have developed my own educated guess, based on extensive research by an educated palate:

In 1784, although not recorded on any documents preserved for posterity, Padre Pablo Mugartegui had a small, private still with which he converted fine California wine, produced in either 1783 or 1784, into great California brandy. And if that is not the case, he was missing an awesomely good beverage.

Happy birthday, California Brandy. And many happy returns.

James R. McManus, President
California Brandy Advisory Board

California's New Spirit
Brandy

California's new spirit - brandy

California brandy, the most versatile spirit in the world, is used in thousands of recipes for drinks, punches and cocktails, as well as for various foods. It is a natural product, distilled from the purest grape wines and aged in wood to bring out the best of its taste and bouquet. Many people consider California brandy to be the most civilized spirit man has created.

It takes more than a ton of grapes to make one barrel of California brandy. All California brandies must be legally aged two years, but most are aged four or more years. The majority of California brandies are blended and each brandymaster has his/her own special formula for attaining perfection.

California over the years has produced over 125 varieties of grapes used for producing brandy. During the first two decades of brandy-making in California the Franciscan fathers used an unknown grape that later became known as the mission variety because it was cultivated around every mission settlement. By the 1860s cuttings from European vines were so plentiful that brandymakers began mixing and experimenting.

Today, Tokay is grown in the northern area of the San Joaquin Valley and Thompson Seedless is favored in the central and southern regions of the state. Both Tokay and Thompson seedless are particularly fragrant and rich in sugar content which is ideal for producing smooth, light brandy that appeals to American palates. Other grapes used for blending include Emperor, Grenache, Malaga, and Petite Sirah.

Brandy - a revolutionary mark of distinction

Samuel Johnson wrote in 1790, "Claret is the liquor for boys. Port for men. But he who aspires to be a hero must drink brandy." Perhaps the inspiration for these words came from an observation of the culinary habits of our country's founding fathers.

George Washington, who kept detailed accounts of the food and drink enjoyed at Mount Vernon, listed brandy as the second most frequently served beverage. Brandy was also a featured ingredient in the Washingtons' acclaimed Christmas desserts: Sweet Potato Pudding, Plum Pudding and Cherry Bounce.

Due to his fondness for brandy Washington kept his cellar well stocked with the spirit. Upon his death, more than 150 gallons were discovered at Mount Vernon.

The first occupants of the White House were as partial to brandy as the Washingtons. John and Abigail Adams often served a Berry Shrub that the president had himself concocted.

Thomas Jefferson, who had a reputation as a gourmet, enjoyed his food smothered with brandy or wine. Jefferson compensated for the lack of central heating in the White House by serving Hot Spiced Toddy, a warming blend of brandy, nutmeg, sugar and baked apples. Brandied peaches was a standard offering at the Jefferson dinner table.

The serving of brandy was a part of the overall tradition of hospitality in the sparsely settled New World. Taverns and inns served as community centers, where local merchants, government officials and townsfolk would meet to discuss the business of politics of the day. Taverns commonly served wine, beer, ale, whiskey, and Jamaican rum. But because brandy was relatively hard to get it was considered a drink for the wealthy, a mark of distinction.

The spirit was held in such high esteem that in 1738 Thomas Jefferson's father, Peter, once sold some land for an undisclosed amount of money and "the consideration of Henry Wetherburn's biggest bowl of Arrack Punch," a local concoction liberally enriched with brandy.

Heroes, hospitality, and brandy are traditionally an important part of this country's history, and this is a tradition that is unlikely to change.

How to taste brandy

The color of California brandy depends upon aging and additives. Generally, the longer the brandy ages in wood the darker it becomes. Most brandymakers, like whiskey producers, add a little carmel to the brandy to produce an amber color without affecting the flavor.

California brandies differ from each other because some have a stronger flavor, while others are more aromatic. Some are drier, while others tend to be sweeter. Degree of fragrance, strength of flavor and other characteristics, depend upon the individual brandymaster's recipe. That is why there is a California brandy for every taste.

Tasting brandy is not as difficult as some people would have you believe. The high alcoholic content in brandy tends to wipe out the thousands of sensitive taste buds in your mouth. This is why professional tasters always wash out their mouths and glasses with water. Rinsing restores the taste buds and keeps the glass from smelling of the last brandy tasted.

Some brandy tasters prefer to mix equal parts of brandy and distilled water together and then taste the brandy. This allows them to taste and swallow a little of the mixture, which they claim permits them to further analyze the brandy.

Here is how to taste California brandy.

First, use a 6-ounce brandy snifter. Make sure the snifter is odorless.

Second, pour one ounce of brandy into the snifter. Now swirl the brandy around and around. This helps the brandy to breathe.

Third, cup your hand underneath the entire bottom of the snifter, with the stem between your middle and ring fingers. Your hand will begin to warm the brandy, thus releasing new aromas.

Fourth, take a quick forceful sniff of the brandy. Do not repeat the process for about 10 seconds. Your olfactory senses are subject to a rapid adaptation to the spirit and can become fatigued.

Fifth, take a little brandy into your mouth and wash it all around your mouth so that all of the taste buds get a chance to taste the brandy. While the brandy is in your mouth, inhale a little air letting it pass over the brandy and into the lungs. With the air still in your lungs, swallow the brandy. Keep your mouth closed and exhale the air from your lungs. The fumes will tell all you need to know about California brandy.

Cooking with brandy

Brandy imparts a special flavor when used in cooking. Whether the brandy is flamed, simmered, stewed or even used to deglaze pans, producing a delicious sauce, it always enhances the final taste of a dish. Cooking with brandy adds a new dimension to your cooking skills and culinary talents. No kitchen should be without a bottle of California brandy.

Brandy was first used as a preservative. It kept foods from spoiling and became a liquid refrigerator for our ancestors' provisions. In their love for spicy dishes, they not only added cinnamon, sugar and anise, but liberally used brandy to perk up their offerings.

It has been only 150 years since flaming dishes with brandy moved from the kitchen into the dining room. Before that, flaming was done in the kitchen and was for some 700 years a "trick of the chef." Culinary archivists tell us that one Christmas Eve an apprentice was unaware that the chef had poured an extra amount of brandy on the plum pudding. While playing with matches, he accidentally set the pudding on fire. He panicked and grabbed the flaming dish, and instead of running into the backyard, he ran into the dining room where he stood motionless as the pudding blazed. Thinking that it was a new dish, the hostess and her guests stood and applauded. The "flambée" was born.

Here are some basic rules you should consider when cooking with brandy.

First, the amount of brandy called for in this cookbook is necessary to make a dish taste a certain way. Since you have your own taste requirements, you should feel free to make the necessary adjustments.

Second, do not be afraid to experiment. Half the fun of cooking is creating new dishes and letting your imagination soar to new heights.

Third, learn how to flame properly. As I travel throughout the United States demonstrating the simple technique of flaming dishes, the number one question I am asked is: "How do I get the brandy to flame?"

The trick to flaming brandy is to heat the amount called for in the recipe in a small saucepan. Heat the brandy until it begins to sizzle, that is when the little bubbles rise from the bottom of the pan to the top of the liquid. This means that the brandy is ready to be flamed. You can either ignite the brandy while it is still in the saucepan or pour the heated brandy into the prepared dish and ignite it. It is just as simple as that.

Lastly, more and more people are enjoying California brandy in food and serving it to their guests. Last year, Americans consumed 259,000 bottles of brandy every day. And of the 259,000 bottles, 178,000 were the brandies of California.

Brandy had been produced by Spanish mission fathers in California since 1784 but it wasn't until the Gold Rush of '49, when the population soared in the western states, that demand for the spirit increased dramatically.

Even Captain John Sutter of gold discovery fame constructed a brandy distillery at Fort Sutter on the American River. Sutter tried to distill the native, wild grapes into brandy but he enjoyed better fortune with gold.

Chapter two
Brandy &
Hors d'Oeuvres

They have been called soakers, blotters, splashers, thumb-bits, starters and canapes. Americans call them appetizers and the French include sitdown first courses and call them hors d'oeuvres.

No matter what you call them, those little morsels are finding their way back onto menus today. With the trend toward lighter eating, they are helping people watch their waistlines. They curb your appetite and thus you don't gorge yourself on other, richer courses.

One of the reasons hors d'oeuvres began to disappear from the gastronomic circuit is their lack of variety. No matter what party you attend, chances are you'll find yourself faced with tiny meatballs in a watery brown canned sauce; little sausages that taste as if they were made from a pig's foot rather than from his hocks; crisp bacon wrapped in chicken livers (a combination that, if the livers are overcooked, and they usually are, destroys one's taste buds) and other tidbits that insult the palate instead of inspiring it.

Before I introduce you to the "real" world of hors d'oeuvres, there are several rules you should keep in mind when planning menus.

- If you plan to serve a heavy dinner, the hors d'oeuvres should be light and consist of not more than three types.
- If you plan a light dinner, then it is reasonable to serve four to six hors d'oeuvres.
- The hors d'oeuvres should never fill the guests to the point where they feel stuffed.
- The best wine for hors d'oeuvres is champagne or a small brandy and soda.

Here are some different hors d'oeuvres that will spark up your menus.

Carpaccio

Man ate his share of raw meat long before he accidentally discovered fire. Warriors of old ate meat raw as a sign of strength. Raw meat was a favorite of the Russian court and that is why steak tartare was so named. The darling of the world of cuisine today is an old Italian hors d'oeuvre, Carpaccio. The way some people rave about it today you would never guess it has been served in Italian households for years.

1-1/2 pounds fat free filet, sliced paper thin
1/2 cup olive oil
1/4 cup red wine vinegar
1/4 cup soy sauce
1/4 cup California brandy
1-1/2 teaspoons salt
1 teaspoon fresh ground black pepper
1 teaspoon thyme
1 large onion, minced
2 cloves garlic, minced

Mix all the ingredients, except the beef, and let stand 15 minutes. Lay the slices of beef on a large tray slightly overlapping each other, about 1/4 of an inch. With a pastry brush, brush the meat with the marinade several times so the meat can absorb some of the liquid. Brush 4 or 5 times every 10 minutes. Garnish the platter with lemon wedges and parsley. Serves 6.

The art of making brandy was introduced to California some 200 years ago by the Franciscan fathers. Within a very short time the fathers were producing brandy for commercial purposes and by 1785 were shipping barrels of brandy around the Horn and back to Spain.

Shrimp fra diavolo

Brandy was not called brandy until the early 1800s. The Franciscan fathers named the beverage "aguardiente," a generic term for any spirit distilled from fruit.

Shrimp is so expensive these days, it is being served as an hors d'oeuvre rather than as a main course. Here is a simple shrimp dish that is inexpensive and whets your company's appetite.

1 pound raw shrimp, shelled and deveined
6 tablespoons grapeseed oil or olive oil
2 cloves garlic, peeled
1/4 cup California brandy
3 tomatoes, peeled, seeded and chopped
1 teaspoon salt
Pinch of dried oregano
Pinch of dried red peppers

Sauté the shrimp and garlic in the oil until the shrimp begins to turn pink. Remove the garlic, add brandy, cover and steam 2 minutes. Add remaining ingredients and cook 15 minutes. Divide the shrimp into 6 equal portions. Serves 6.

Mushrooms montebello

With people watching their waistlines these days, fruits and vegetables are the "in" thing. Here is a veggie dish that can be served as an hors d'oeuvre.

1/2 pound fresh mushrooms, small button kind
1/2 teaspoon crushed oregano
Salt and pepper to taste
1/4 cup olive oil
1 clove garlic, crushed
1 tablespoon California brandy
2 tablespoons red wine vinegar
Pinch of dill weed

Cut the stems from the mushrooms and reserve for another use. (They can be chopped fine, mixed with mayonnaise and used as a spread.) Wash the caps, dry and cut in half. Mix remaining ingredients in a bowl. Add mushrooms, toss well and let marinate for at least 1 hour. Serve with toothpicks. Serves 6.

Barbequed wings

Chicken wings, when properly prepared, are one of the better hors d'oeuvres you can serve your guests. And the addition of some California brandy gives the wings a special taste. Again, this dish lends itself to either indoor or outdoor cooking.

16 chicken wings
2/3 cup tomato paste
1/4 cup molasses
1/4 cup California brandy
1/4 cup cider vinegar
2 tablespoons peanut oil
1-1/2 tablespoons Dijon mustard
2 cloves garlic, minced
2 teaspoons Worcestershire sauce
1/2 teaspoon Tabasco sauce

When the Franciscan padres came to California in 1769, they designed their missions and the surrounding land to include vineyards which would supply them with altar wines and, of course, brandy.

Set the wings aside and mix remaining ingredients. Lay the wings in a shallow pan and pour the mixture over them. Marinate for at least 1 hour, turning the wings so they are well coated. Transfer the wings with a slotted spoon to the charcoal grill or oven broiler and cook 10 minutes on each side, basting the wings with the remaining sauce. Divide the wings evenly and top with some of the sauce. Serves 4.

Skewered beef

This is an all around hors d'oeuvre, because it can be served all year. It is at home under the oven broiler or over the charcoal barbecue.

36 paper thin slices of beef
2 cups of your favorite salad dressing
1/4 cup California brandy
18 bamboo skewers

Put the beef slices in a glass bowl. Add the salad dressing and brandy. Marinate for at least 2 hours. Place six slices of the beef on each skewer. Broil or grill one minute on each side. CHEF'S NOTE: The thinner you slice the beef the faster it will cook. Serves 6.

By 1823, there were 21 Franciscan missions established in California. All established vineyards and all but four were successful at making wine and brandy.

Rillettes au california

I don't know why more people do not serve this little pork paté. It is easy to make, exceptionally tasty and can be kept several weeks in the refrigerator or several months in the freezer. Moreover, it is handy for the unexpected company that sometimes drops over.

1 pound fresh pork, diced
1 pound fresh salt pork, blanched and diced
1/4 teaspoon cinnamon
1/4 teaspoon freshly grated nutmeg
1 whole bay leaf
1 sprig thyme
1 large sprig parsley
1 clove garlic, unpeeled
2 whole cloves
1/4 cup California brandy
Water to cover

Put the first four ingredients in a 3-quart saucepan. In a cheesecloth bag, put the bay leaf, thyme, parsley, garlic and cloves. Tie together and put into the saucepan. Add brandy and water to cover. Cook 1 hour. Strain meats through a fine strainer. Reserve liquid. Discard cheesecloth bag. Put the meats through a food processor and whirl on and off until the meat is puréed. If the mixture is too dry, add some of the reserved liquid. Pack into 2-quart or 2-cup souffle molds. Serves 6.

Toast ronald

1 slice of French or Italian bread, 1/2 inch thick
1 tablespoon butter
1 dash red pepper flakes
1 pinch fennel seeds
5 dashes California brandy
2 tablespoons grated Mozzarella cheese

Butter the bread. Add pepper flakes, fennel seeds, brandy and cover with cheese. Put under the broiler for one minute or until the cheese is bubbling and just ready to turn brown. Cut in half. Serves 1.

California brandy spread

Many years ago, a New York restaurant offered watercress sandwiches every day to its customers before dinner or before they had to catch a train home. They were the perfect hors d'oeuvres because they were small, went well with most before-dinner drinks and, if you had a long train ride home, helped curb your appetite. Here is another simple hors d'oeuvre—a brandy spread that you can make, keep and serve whenever the need arises.

1/4 cup California brandy
1 cup diced ham
1 cup cooked chicken livers
1 hard boiled egg
1 cup mayonnaise
Salt and white pepper to taste

Mix all the above ingredients in a food processor or blender until smooth. Pack in small jars. Spread on any of your favorite breads. Serves 6.

Father Narciso Durán of the Mission San José provided consultation on wine and brandy to the governor of Mexican California in 1833. He wrote that the best wines and brandy of the missions were those of San Gabriel. He recommended a delicious dessert drink made from the unfermented juice of white grapes mixed with brandy . . . "it would shine at the table of the president of the Republic for smoothness, delicacy and simplicity of composition . . ."

Brandy roquefort spread

Here is another spread which appeared in my *First Brandy Cookbook*. It has received wide recognition as an excellent recipe and, since the book is out of print, I have reprinted it here.

1 pound Roquefort cheese, room temperature
1/2 pound butter, room temperature
1/3 cup California brandy
Pinch of cayenne pepper
1/4 cup onions, minced

Mix the cheese and butter together with a fork or place in a food processor or blender. Add brandy, pepper and onions. Mix well into a smooth paste. Can be served on your favorite breads or crackers. Makes 3 cups.

Chapter three
Brandy & Soup

oups are a chef's calling card. If the soup is good, well made and you want a second bowl, that restaurant's food will probably be excellent. However, if the soup is thin, watery and tasteless, leave at once.

The best soups are made from stocks, homemade stocks, if that is possible. The next best is canned stocks, which are fine when the busy cook just doesn't have 10 hours to make a chicken, beef or veal stock. Even if homemade stocks are not available, fresh ingredients that can be added to a canned stock are available in any store in the United States. And they should be used.

Soups are versatile. Just about anything can be put into a pot with some stock or water and cooked to become a soup. There is an old story about soup, one of the most charming stories ever written.

Once upon a time a stranger came to town. In the middle of the town square he set up a large kettle over a roaring fire. He filled the kettle with water and from his robe took a large nail and dropped it into the kettle. When asked what he was doing, the stranger replied, "I am making nail soup."

The townspeople gathered about him to watch. He tasted the water with the nail in it and said, "How much better this soup would taste if I had an old bone to put into the pot." Someone in the crowd produced a bone and the stranger dropped the bone into the pot. He tasted the soup again and expressed the thought that a carrot would add much flavor. An onlooker gave him a carrot. He tasted the soup again and mused that perhaps a piece of meat, a clove of garlic and a stalk of celery would certainly help. All were offered for the pot.

Pronouncing the soup ready, he let the townspeople taste it. They all nodded their heads saying, "Yes, you can make a good soup from a nail."

It is too bad the stranger didn't know about California brandy, for the addition of a little brandy would have made a big difference.

Lentil soup hébert

Bean soups are among the most favored soups both in the United States and in Europe. They are filling, are a good source of fiber, and lend themselves to many variations on a theme. Beans soups have played an important part in both royalty and music. Queen Elizabeth I and Queen Victoria were very fond of sipping a bean and broth soup at breakfast, which they claimed stimulated their appetites and helped them face their regal duties for the remainder of the day.

Paderewski, Stokowski and Verdi all loved bean soups. Ignace Paderewski and Leopold Stokowski loved bean soup for breakfast, while the great Italian composer Guiseppe Verdi, gracefully attributed much of his operatic inspiration to the warming and sustaining effects of a large bowl of bean soup.

Here is my favorite bean soup, a special lentil soup, that is made quickly and easily in a pressure cooker.

1 cup dry lentils
2 cups chicken stock
2 cups water
1/4 cup salt pork, diced and blanched
1/2 cup carrots, grated
1 cup onions, diced
1 clove garlic, crushed
1 bay leaf
Salt and pepper to taste
1 tomato, peeled and chopped
1/4 cup California brandy

Put the lentils, stock and water in a pressure cooker and let soak overnight. The next morning add remaining ingredients and cook 10 minutes in the pressure cooker. Serves 6.

U.S. Senator, George Hearst acquired the Madrone Vineyard of Sonoma Valley in 1885. He perfected the vineyards and brandy making and proudly served his California brandy to international guests in Washington D.C.

Onion soup

Onion soup without the addition of brandy is just not onion soup. There is nothing more invigorating than a bowl of hot onion soup laced with brandy to sooth the inner person and get one going again. I have always loved onion soup and I guess if I were marooned on a desert island and had only one soup to survive on, I would choose onion soup plus a bottle of California brandy.

Here is an easy onion soup recipe, one that can be made in 20 minutes and, if frozen, keeps several months.

3 cups sliced onions, Italian red, if possible
1/2 cup butter
Salt and black pepper to taste
1-1/2 quarts rich beef stock
1/4 cup California brandy
1/2 cup freshly grated Parmesan cheese

Sauté the onions over very high heat so they get a little carmel tinge on their edges. Lower heat and sauté until the onions are soft. Add stock and brandy and cook another 10 minutes. Serve in deep soup bowls and pass the cheese. Serves 6.

Brandy consommé

One of the simplest of soups is a rich beef consommé plus the addition of California brandy, served piping hot. The garnish is minced parsley or minced hard boiled eggs.

6 cups consommé, homemade if possible
2 tablespoons California brandy
Minced parsley or minced hard boiled egg

Heat the consommé very hot. Add brandy. Served topped with parsley or egg. Serves 6.

Creamed onion soup

My ancestors come from the Normandy penisula in France. There the people use cream, butter and a Norman apple brandy called Calvados in much of their cooking. It was there that I first tasted a special onion soup made with butter and cream. Gastronomic historians suggest that such a creamed onion soup dates back to the 18th century, but I suspect that it had been made hundreds of years before the 18th century. Why? Because the butter, cream and brandy of Normandy have been world renowned for some 1,000 years. In this recipe, I have used California brandy instead of the French Calvados.

Brandy improves with age. The older I get, the more I like it.
—ANONYMOUS

10 tablespoons sweet butter
6 cups onions, sliced
8 cups beef stock
1/4 cup California brandy
Salt and black pepper to taste
2 egg yolks
1/2 cup heavy (whipping) cream
5 or 6 slices French or Italian bread, toasted
Cheese of your choice

In a soup kettle, melt the butter and sauté the onions on low heat for 20 minutes. Add beef broth and simmer 10 more minutes. Add brandy, salt and pepper. Beat yolks with cream until mixed. Add a little of the hot soup, beating with a whisk constantly. Slowly pour the yolk and cream mixture back into the soup kettle, whisking constantly. Put a slice of the bread in each soup bowl and add the soup. Pass the cheese. Serves 6.

New england clam chowder

Clam chowder is a soup that has been an American favorite ever since the Pilgrims landed in Jamestown. The first Americans found such an abundance of clams on the shores that they ate as many of them as possible and in as many forms as possible. But it was clam chowder that they loved best. This recipe dates back to those early times.

1 cup salt pork, diced and blanched
1 large onion, chopped fine
2 6-1/2-ounce cans minced clams
8-ounce bottle clam juice
1 cup water
1/4 cup California brandy
4 potatoes, peeled and diced
1 bay leaf
Salt and white pepper to taste
2 cups whole milk

Sauté pork until soft. Add onions and cook until soft. Add clams, their juice, bottled clam juice, water, potatoes, bay leaf, salt and pepper. Cook until potatoes are done. Add milk. Reheat. Serves 4.

Virginia pumpkin soup

It is a well known fact that if it hadn't been for the American Indians, the Pilgrims would have starved to death. The Indians taught the colonists how to grow sweet corn, beans, squash and pumpkins. Captain John Smith noted in his journal that during the first winter in Virginia, "...we feasted daily with good bread, peas and pumpkin as well as fish and fowl." One of the staples in those days was soup and there is no question that pumpkin soup was one such weekly offering.

1/4 cup sweet butter
1/2 cup onions, minced
1/4 teaspoon fresh grated nutmeg
3-1/2 cups chicken stock
2-1/2 cups canned pumpkin
1 cup half and half
4 tablespoons California brandy
Salt and pepper to taste

Sauté the onions in the butter in a large saucepan and cook until soft. Add nutmeg and stock. Bring to the boil. Add pumpkin, half and half, brandy, and salt and pepper. Heat mixture and simmer 10 minutes. Serves 8.

Brandied chestnut soup

Here is a different kind of soup that uses puréed chestnuts as a special flavoring agent. Chestnut purée can be found in cans today so there is no need to make your own. In addition, you can pour this soup into a thermos and take it along on a picnic.

2 tablespoons butter
3 carrots, washed and minced
2 stalks celery, chopped
1 small onion, chopped
2 10-1/2-ounce cans chicken stock
4 cups water
1 cup dry white wine
15-ounce can chestnut purée
1/2 teaspoon ground cloves
1/2 cup heavy (whipping) cream
1/4 cup California brandy
Salt and pepper to taste
Sour cream
Parsley, minced

There are more than 200 brands of California brandy marketed in the United States today. Brands differ from one to another in color, body and flavor.

Melt the butter in a large kettle and sauté the carrots, celery and onions for 10 minutes or until they are soft. Add stock, wine and water. Bring to the boil, then lower heat and simmer for 2 hours, covered. Strain the stock, reserving the vegetables. Return the vegetables to the kettle, add 4 cups of the stock and the cloves. Cover and simmer 20 minutes. Purée the soup in a food processor or blender. Return the mixture to the kettle and add the chestnut purée, cream, brandy and bring to the simmer. Add salt and pepper. When ready to serve, add a dollop of sour cream and a little parsley to each bowl. Serves 6.

Brandied zucchini soup

It is amazing how zucchini has taken off as a vegetable. Its popularity has zoomed in the past decade and there seems to be no end to the number of ways it can be prepared. Here is a special chilled soup that is best as a warm weather luncheon entrée or as a beginning to a evening meal; of course, it features zucchini.

1/4 cup onions, chopped
2 tablespoons butter
10-1/2-ounce can chicken stock
1 pound zucchini, sliced
1 tablespoon flour
2 cups whole milk
1/3 cup California brandy
Salt and white pepper to taste
1 cup half and half

Sauté the onions in half the butter and cook until they are soft. Add stock and zucchini. Heat to the boil, cover and simmer 15 minutes. Pour the mixture into a food processor or blender and blend until smooth. Melt remaining butter and stir in the flour. Add the milk, brandy, salt and pepper. Heat to the boil, stirring constantly. Add half and half and zucchini mixture. Mix well. Chill. Serves 6.

Apple soup

Cold fruit soups have been a part of the cuisine of the world for hundreds of years. Many cold soups have been served as a dessert course. Yet the people in the Scandinavian countries often serve them as a soup course, especially when various fruits are in season. They can wake up dull taste buds and get you set for the next course.

1-1/2 pounds apples, peeled, cored and cut into small cubes
Water to cover
Sugar to taste (optional)
Juice of 1 lemon
1/4 cup California brandy

In a saucepan, simmer the apples in the water along with the sugar and lemon juice. The apples should be soft in 15-20 minutes. Press them through a sieve and add brandy. Refrigerate the soup until very cold. Serves 4.

Chapter four
Brandy & Fowl

Chickens, capons, cornish game hens, pheasant, quail, grouse, partridge, turkey, geese, ducks; they all are enhanced when married with California brandy. There is a special something that happens when fowl and brandy get together, a special taste unfolds and we are better off with it than without it.

Man's association with chicken began around 2,000 B.C. in India, where the wild red jungle fowl was first domesticated. The chicken then traveled to China and on to the Pacific Islands, reaching Europe about 1,500 B.C. By 720 B.C., the bird was being feasted upon by the Greeks, and by 185 B.C. the Romans were enjoying chicken. A hundred years later the chicken was firmly established in the kitchens of the world.

Chicken is a versatile food. It is good broiled, roasted, baked, steamed, fried, boiled, fricasseed, barbecued, or made into a pie or soup. It has been flavored, stuffed, basted and garnished with almost every food: anise, apples, bacon, beans, cinnamon, cornmeal, crabs, crayfish, eels, fennel, ginger, grape jelly—well, the list goes on and on.

Here are a couple of tips when buying chicken or any fowl for that matter.

- *Always buy a whole chicken and cut it up yourself. If you can't or won't cut it up, buy a whole chicken and ask your butcher to cut it up for you. Your chicken will taste better fresh cut.*
- *If chicken is on sale, buy several whole ones and freeze them.*

Chicken breasts escoffier

Auguste Escoffier was one of the great French chefs who resided in America and did a lot to help Americans appreciate fine cooking. The recipes he left behind for all chefs are masterpieces of cuisine and are still used in hundreds of restaurants throughout the United States. He created many dishes, but I am not sure who created this next dish and named it after him.

By law, all California brandy must be made exclusively from grapes grown in California and must be aged for a minimum of two years. Most California brandies are aged at least four years, while some go as high as 10 years of age.

6 whole chicken breasts, boned, skinned and halved
1/2 cup butter, plus 4 tablespoons
1/2 cup California brandy
1 pound mushrooms, sliced
24 small boiling onions
Salt and pepper
1 bay leaf
1 sprig of thyme
4 cups white wine
2 tablespoons cornstarch
2 tablespoons water
1 cup heavy (whipping) cream

In a pan, sauté the breasts in 1/2 cup butter. When they are brown all over, heat the brandy to the sizzle, pour it over the breasts and ignite. In a separate saucepan, sauté the mushrooms and onions in the remaining butter for 10 minutes or until the mushrooms are tender. Add the mixture to the chicken. Sprinkle the chicken with salt and pepper and add bay leaf, thyme and wine. Cover and cook 20 minutes. Mix the cornstarch and water together to make a smooth paste. Add to the mixture and stir. When well mixed, add cream and stir again. Serves 12.

Chicken in curry & brandy

If you like the taste of curry, this is the chicken dish for you. There are many blends of curries so you might want to try several kinds before you decide on your favorite.

4-pound chicken, cut up
6 tablespoons grapeseed oil or clarified butter
2 onions, sliced
Salt and pepper to taste
2 tablespoons flour
1 tablespoon curry powder
1 cup heavy (whipping) cream
1/3 cup California brandy

In a large skillet heat the oil or butter very hot and add the chicken pieces, onions and salt and pepper. Reduce heat, cover and simmer for 20 minutes or until the chicken is tender. Remove chicken to a warm platter and keep warm in slack oven. Mix the flour and curry together and add the mixture to the skillet. Cook 1 minute. Add cream and brandy and cook until the sauce thickens. Return chicken to the sauce and simmer 10 minutes. Serves 6.

Chicken pietro

Here is a light luncheon dish, one that demands just a simple salad, a glass of white wine and a demitasse of coffee with a small snifter of California brandy.

4-pound chicken, cut up
6 tablespoons grapeseed oil or clarified butter
1/4 cup California brandy
1 cup mushrooms, sliced
3 tablespoons butter
1 cup white wine
1-1/2 cups whipped cream
Salt and white pepper to taste

Sauté the chicken in the oil or butter until brown all over. Heat the brandy to the sizzle, pour over chicken and ignite. Cover, reduce heat and cook 30 minutes. In a separate saucepan, lightly cook the mushrooms in the butter. Combine the chicken and mushrooms on a serving platter. Mix the juices from both pans into one. Add wine and bring to the boil. Lower heat and add whipped cream. Salt and pepper to taste. Pour sauce over chicken. Serves 6.

Chicken hunter style

Here is an old French dish with as many variations as there are Frenchmen. This recipe is sort of a composite of several recipes as it uses the best parts of each.

4-pound chicken, cut in pieces
1/2 cup flour, plus 2 tablespoons
Salt and pepper to taste
4 tablespoons clarified butter
3 onions, minced
1 cup mushrooms, sliced
1/4 cup California brandy
2 cups chicken stock
3 tablespoons tomato paste
2/3 cup white wine
1 bay leaf
2 sprigs parsley
2 tablespoons butter

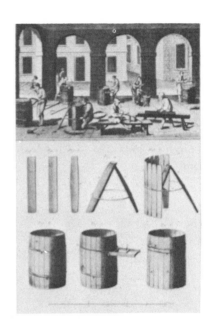

Flour, salt and pepper the chicken pieces. Sauté them in the clarified butter until they are brown all over. Add onions and mushrooms. When onions are soft, heat the brandy to the sizzle. Pour over the chicken and ignite. Mix the stock, paste and wine together and add to the mixture. Add bay leaf and parsley. Bring to the boil. Cover and simmer 45 minutes. Mix the butter with the remaining 2 tablespoons of flour. Arrange the chicken pieces on a warm platter. Gradually mix in the butter/flour combination, stirring well to make sure the sauce thickens properly. Pour sauce over chicken. Serves 6.

Chicken christopher

This recipe appeared in my *First Brandy Cookbook* and received good notices. It is easy to make—in fact, it makes itself.

4-pound chicken, cut up
Salt and pepper to taste
3 tablespoons butter
1/4 cup California brandy
Pinch of dill weed

Salt and pepper the chicken pieces. Melt the butter in a heavy skillet or large casserole and sauté the chicken until it is brown. Heat brandy, ignite and pour over chicken. Cover and cook 20 minutes. Sprinkle with dill. Serves 4.

Chicken pizzaiola

Once in Rome, I tasted a special chicken dish and had to have the recipe. The chef was gracious, named a few ingredients and left it at that. Even Mario, my waiter, threw up his hands and said he couldn't get the recipe. So I went back a few more times and ordered the same dish. Here is my version and I think it is as close as one can come to duplicating the original.

2 whole chicken breasts, boned, skinned and halved
1 egg yolk, beaten
1/2 cup flour
4 tablespoons butter
1/4 cup California brandy
1 recipe Pizzaiola sauce (see below)
6 tablespoons heavy (whipping) cream
1 cup toasted croutons

Dip the breasts in the yolk and then flour and sauté them in the butter until brown all over. Add brandy and cook 3 minutes. Add sauce and cream and simmer 20 minutes. Put mixture on a warm platter and top with croutons. Serves 4.

Pizzaiola sauce

4 tablespoons olive oil
1 clove garlic, minced
10-ounce can tomatoes
1 tablespoon dried oregano
Salt and pepper to taste

Heat the oil in a saucepan. When very hot, add garlic and cook 30 seconds. Turn off heat and let cool for 30 more seconds. Add remaining ingredients and simmer 20 minutes. Yield 1-1/2 cups.

Chicken pot-au-feu

This chicken recipe is ideal for one pot cookery. It is an adaption of the French pot-au-feu dish which is so popular among the country people of France.

3-1/3 pound chicken, with giblets
1/4 cup onion, chopped
1/2 cup celery, chopped with tops
2/3 cup California brandy
3 10-1/2-ounce cans chicken stock
3 cups water
1 tablespoon salt
1 bay leaf
3/4 pound boiling onions
2 cups carrots, sliced
2 cups zucchini, thickly sliced
1 cup celery, sliced
1 tablespoon parsley, minced

California's first full-time wine and brandymaker was Jean Louis Vignes who had been exiled from his native France for unknown reasons in 1826. Arriving in the pueblo of Los Angeles when he was 53 years old, he almost immediately planted a vineyard that eventually produced enough wine and brandy to distribute to settlements along the California coast.

Place giblets, onion and celery inside the chicken. Add 2 tablespoons of the brandy and skewer opening. Place chicken, breast side down in a deep kettle large enough to hold the bird. Add stock, water, salt and bay leaf. Cover and simmer 20 minutes. Turn chicken breast side up, cover and cook another 20 minutes. Add boiling onions and sliced carrots to the broth and cook 10 minutes. Add zucchini, celery and remaining brandy and simmer 5-8 minutes more, just until the vegetables are tender. Add parsley. Remove the chicken to a serving casserole. Pour hot soup around the chicken. Serves 6. CHEF'S NOTE: You can serve this dish in two courses. The first course is soup and the second course is the chicken with the vegetables. If you want, you can serve everything at once in large soup bowls.

Roast chicken

One of the best ways to cook chicken is to roast it. This method is very old, so old that gastronomic historians are not sure just when man first switched from raw meat to roasted meat. This next recipe uses two of my favorite spirits: California brandy and port wine.

4-pound roasting chicken
Salt and pepper to taste
4 ounces butter
1 rib of celery, cut in thirds
3/4 cup California brandy
1/2 cup port wine
2 tablespoons heavy (whipping) cream

Rub the chicken inside and out with salt and pepper. Place the butter and celery inside the chicken. Put the chicken on a rack and roast it at 425 degrees for 25 minutes. Heat the brandy to the sizzle, pour it over the chicken and ignite. Baste the chicken until the flame dies. Add port and cream and return chicken to the oven, lowering the temperature to 325 degrees. When cooked, carve and serve with the pan juices. Serves 6.

Pheasant my way

Pheasant is again plentiful. It has been domesticated but is expensive when you can find it. If you are lucky to have a hunter in the house or a friend who will share an extra bird with you, I suggest you try this recipe.

1/4 cup butter
1/2 cup onions, minced
3 pheasants
1/2 cup California brandy
2 cups chicken stock
Salt and pepper to taste
6 slices non-smoked bacon
2 cups heavy (whipping) cream
1/4 cup horseradish

Sauté the onions in the butter in a large sauté pan. It should be large enough to hold the three pheasants; if not, use a roasting pan. Add pheasants and sauté over high heat for 15 minutes. Heat the brandy to the sizzle, ignite and pour over the birds. Then add stock, salt and pepper. Put bacon slices over the breasts and roast in a 375 degree oven for 45 minutes, basting the birds every 10 minutes with the pan juices. Add cream and horseradish to the pan juices and stir to mix well. Serve pheasants with pan juices. Serves 6.

Jean Louis Vignes, came from France at age 9 and settled in Los Angeles in the 1830s. He established a large vineyard and is acclaimed by some as the "father of the California wine industry". He gained a fine reputation for his brandy which was described in William Heath Davis's book, SEVENTY FIVE YEARS IN CALIFORNIA: "a superior article when three or four years old. Beyond that, it still further improved in quality, being of a fine flavor, entirely pure, and was regarded as a wholesome drink."

Hens with mushrooms & brandy

Rock Cornish Game Hens burst onto the culinary scene some 30 years ago. They were developed by a Connecticut breeder in the late 1950s. He crossed a Plymouth Rock with a Cornish Game Cock. The latter is a descendent of the famed Malayan game cock, one of the most ferocious of man's feathered friends.

The Rock Cornish Game Hen is a little butterball of a bird when you consider that he has large plump breasts, stubby legs and provides an enormous amount of good eating.

Cornish hens are tender and eatable because they are brought to the market when they are just six weeks old. They weigh between a pound and 18 ounces.

The fresh hens are the best. Many stores now carry the fresh hens and if they don't, they can get them. In the following recipes, I have allowed one hen for two people but for hungry people, one hen per person should fill the bill.

3 Rock Cornish Game Hens, split in half
Salt and pepper to taste
1/2 teaspoon marjoram
1 pound mushrooms, quartered
1/4 cup butter, plus 2 tablespoons
1/4 cup California brandy
1 tablespoon parsley, minced

Sprinkle salt, pepper and marjoram on both sides of the split hens. Broil the hens 10 minutes on each side. In a saucepan, sauté the mushrooms in the 1/4 cup butter until soft. Add remaining butter and brandy and cook 2 minutes. Arrange the hens on a serving platter. Pour the sauce over the hens. Top with parsley. Serves 6.

Hens flambés

Every so often, you have to serve an elegant dish at the table. And, of course, it should be flaming, enticing and tasteful.

1 onion, minced
2 tablespoons butter
1/2 cup diced ham
1/2 cup diced mushrooms
1-1/2 cups cooked rice
1/2 cup California brandy
Pinch each of marjoram and thyme
6 Rock Cornish Game Hens
Salt and pepper to taste
1/2 cup chicken stock
1/4 cup sherry

Sauté the onion in the butter until they are soft. Add ham, mushrooms and cook another 5 minutes. Remove the mixture from the stove and add the rice, 1/4 cup of the brandy, the marjoram and thyme. Sprinkle the hens inside and out with the salt and pepper. Divide the stuffing in 6 equal parts and stuff the cavities. Lay the hens side by side in a buttered shallow casserole. Roast in a 350 degree oven for 40 minutes, basting the hens with the pan juices. If the hens are not brown enough on the outside, raise the oven temperature to 450 degrees. When done, remove the hens to a warm serving platter. Add the stock and sherry and cook 5 minutes. Strain the sauce over hens. At the table, heat the remaining 1/4 cup brandy to the sizzle. Pour the heated brandy over the hens, ignite and let it burn until the flame dies out. Serves 6-8.

Chicken breasts with brandy

If you are a "home by six, dinner by seven" person, here is an excellent chicken dish that is easy to prepare, but tastes as if you cooked all day.

3 whole chicken breasts, boned, skinned and halved
4 tablespoons grapeseed oil or olive oil
1/4 cup California brandy
1/2 cup white wine or Madeira wine
3/4 cup chicken stock

Sauté the breasts in the oil until almost done. Heat the brandy to the sizzle, pour it over the breasts and ignite. Cover and cook the breasts 5 more minutes. Remove the breasts to a warm platter and keep warm in a slack oven. Deglaze the hot pan with the wine and add stock. Cook over high heat and reduce to half its volume. Strain and pour over breasts. Serves 6.

Anitra

Italians love duck. In the restaurants in Rome, Milan, Florence and Venice, duck is served in many ways, as it is in many Italian homes. When you are in Italy and you order "anitra," you will get duck.

6-pound duck, cut up
Salt and pepper to taste
2 onions, chopped
2 teaspoons parsley, minced
1 bay leaf
Large pinch of thyme
1/4 cup California brandy
1 clove garlic, minced
2 cups red wine
1/4 cup olive oil
1/2 pound mushrooms, quartered

Sprinkle the duck pieces with the salt and pepper. Put the duck in a deep non-metal dish and add the onions, parsley, bay leaf, thyme, garlic, brandy and red wine. Marinate at least 4 hours. Put the oil in a casserole and heat over a high heat. Take duck pieces from marinade and brown the duck in oil for 10-12 minutes. Add reserved marinade and mushrooms. Cover and simmer for 1 hour or until the duck is tender. Serves 4-6.

Honeyed hens

I think this recipe is Moorish in nature because of the use of honey mixed with butter. Nevertheless, it is best served with rice and a bottle of champagne.

6 Rock Cornish Game Hens
Salt and pepper to taste
1 pound smoked bacon
4 ounces honey
3 ounces butter
1/4 cup California brandy

Salt and pepper the hens inside and out. Put hens in a shallow, buttered casserole and top them with the slices of bacon. Melt the honey and butter and pour it over the hens. Roast the hens at 400 degrees in the oven for 1 hour. When ready to serve, heat the brandy to the sizzle, ignite and pour over hens. Serves 6.

Cajun duck

The ducks we are getting today are some of the finest being raised. There are still some people who like the taste of wild duck, but wild ducks are getting harder and harder to come by. The people of Louisiana, especially the Cajun people, love duck. They have many ways of preparing it and this one is with California brandy.

A good claim can be made for brandy as being the world's oldest spirit. Historical records document that brandy was being produced by the French and Irish back in the 10th century and there is speculation that it was first distilled from rice wine by the Chinese around 800 B.C.

5- or 6-pound duck, cut up
1/4 cup California brandy
1 cup dry red wine
2 onions, chopped
1 tablespoon parsley, minced
1/2 teaspoon dried thyme
1/2 teaspoon dried marjoram
1/4 teaspoon allspice
1 bay leaf, broken in small pieces
Salt and pepper to taste
3 tablespoons clarified butter
3 tablespoons grapeseed oil or olive oil
1 garlic clove, minced
3/4 cup beef stock

Put the duck pieces in a marinade made of the brandy, wine, onions, parsley, thyme, marjoram, allspice and bay leaf. Marinate the duck 5 or more hours in a non-metal bowl. Cover with plastic wrap and place in the refrigerator. When ready to cook the duck, remove from marinade and strain the marinade and reserve. In a heavy skillet, heat the oils until they are very hot. Sauté the duck pieces and cook 15 minutes until they are brown all over. Add garlic, 1/2 cup of the marinade and the beef stock. Cover and simmer until the duck is tender, about 1 to 1-1/2 hours. Serve right from the skillet. Spoon some of the sauce over each piece of duck. Serves 4-6.

Spit roasted duck

Like chicken, roasted duck is delicious. And the less done to the duck as it is roasting, the better.

6-pound duck
Juice of 1 large lemon
Salt and black pepper to taste
1/4 cup butter, melted
1/2 cup California brandy

Rub the duck with the lemon juice and season it with the salt and pepper. Put the duck on a spit and roast it over coals for 20 minutes or more depending upon the heat of your coals. You can also spit-roast the duck in your oven if it is so equipped. Mix the butter and 1/4 cup of brandy together and baste the duck every 6-7 minutes which will produce a dark, crisp, brown skin. Just before serving, heat the remaining 1/4 cup of brandy to the sizzle, ignite and pour over the duck. Serves 4.

Duck nicoise

In the south of France the word "nicoise" means cooked with garlic, tomatoes and olives, either green or black. This is an excellent and easy dish to cook and serve.

5-pound duck
Salt and black pepper to taste
1 clove garlic, minced
4 tomatoes, peeled, seeded and chopped
1/2 cup green olives, pitted
2 tablespoons parsley, minced
1/2 cup white wine
1/4 cup California brandy
1/4 cup chicken stock
1/2 teaspoon sugar (optional)

Salt and pepper the duck. Truss and place on a rack in a roasting pan. Bake at 325 degrees for 1-1/2 hours or until the duck is brown and cooked. Place the duck on a warm platter and keep it warm. Drain fat from pan. Add remaining ingredients to the pan and cook 10 minutes to reduce the mixture to a thick sauce. Serve sauce with carved duck. Serves 4-6.

California's first American-born viticulturist was a New Englander named Joseph Chapman who came to the West Coast in 1810 after having been pressed into service on a pirate ship. Chapman participated in raids on Mexican California coastal missions and villages until he jumped ship in 1818. After he moved to Mission San Gabriel for asylum he used his blacksmith skills in the winery and distillery and in 1826 he planted 4,000 vines near the pueblo of Los Angeles that were used to produce brandy.

Sautéed quail

Quail farms have sprouted up all over the United States in the past decade. Domesticated quail does not have that gamey taste wild quail has and therefore probably appeals to the majority of people. Farm-bred quail is available in many specialty shops in the United States. If your favorite shop doesn't carry it, ask them to special order it and get some for you. Because quail is so small, allow one whole per person.

6 quail
1/4 cup butter
1/4 cup grapeseed oil or olive oil
1 teaspoon salt
6 grinds fresh nutmeg
3/4 cup white wine
1/2 cup California brandy
1 cup seedless white grapes
6 slices toast, buttered

Heat the butter and oil in a large skillet until very hot. Sauté the quail and brown on all sides. When brown, sprinkle with salt, dust with the nutmeg and add the wine. Reduce heat, cover and simmer the quail for 10 minutes. Remove cover. Heat the brandy to the sizzle, ignite and pour over the birds. When the flame dies out, add the grapes and simmer an additional 10 minutes. Place each quail on the toast with the grapes as a garnish. Serves 6.

Quail flambé

Many times the simplest dishes taste best, like this quickly cooked and flamed quail.

1 quail
Salt and pepper to taste
1/3 cup clarified butter or olive oil
2 tablespoons California brandy
1/4 cup white wine

Salt and pepper the quail. Truss it if you like. Heat the butter or oil in a sauté pan and brown the bird evenly all over, basting it for 10 minutes. Heat the brandy to the sizzle, ignite and pour it over the quail. Add the wine, cover and simmer for another 10 minutes. Serve the quail with the sauce. Serves 1.

Chapter five
Brandy &
Meat

In my 25 years of collecting recipes calling for the use of brandy, I guess beef leads the way with chicken a close second. Certain beef dishes, such as steak with crushed peppercorns, called "Steak au Poivre" in French, has many different versions, as many as the human imagination can devise. I have 17 different ways you can prepare steak with crushed peppercorns and each is slightly different from the other.

In my research, I have discovered what I think may be the original steak and peppercorn recipe. I would like to share it with you and present some creations by other chefs, still using the three basic ingredients: steak, peppercorns and brandy.

Stufato alla trastevere

There is no more popular dish in the world of beef than a good beef stew. It matters little if it has a French name like Boeuf Bourguignonne, or Italian like Stufato alla Manza or a Spanish name like Estofado. What matters is the final taste of the dish.

     A few years ago, I found myself on a plane from Paris to Rome. I had to be in Paris for a writing assignment and had a few extra days to kill. I decided to visit the Eternal City. Within an hour after landing and making hotel arrangements, I was off to the famed Trastevere, which is the old city, a sort of French left bank. Here is made one of the best beef stews you will ever taste. I was fortunate to obtain the recipe from the restaurant owner, whose name I promised not to reveal. But I will share his recipe with you.

1 medium Italian red onion, diced
2 cloves garlic, minced
1/2 pound salt pork, cut in 1/4-inch pieces
2-1/2 pounds beef chuck, cut in 1/2-inch pieces
1/4 teaspoon fresh ground pepper
1/2 teaspoon rosemary, crushed
1/2 teaspoon marjoram, crushed
3 cups red wine
6-ounce can tomato paste
1/4 cup California brandy

In a large pan, cook the first three ingredients for 5 minutes. Add the beef, pepper, rosemary and marjoram. Cook 3 minutes, turning the meat over once or twice. Mix red wine with the tomato paste. Pour in the pan. Add brandy. Stir well. Cook covered for 1 hour, or until the meat is tender. Serves 6.

No poem was ever written by a drinker of water.
                —HORACE

Steak au poivre

This is what I believe to be the original steak with crushed peppercorn recipe. It appeared some 35 years ago in one of the early issues of *Gourmet* magazine. Twenty five years later, all the food and wine writers started raving about it as if it were something new. It wasn't. I have been serving it to my friends and guests for the past 20 years.

1 large steak, 2 inches thick
1 tablespoon course salt
3 tablespoons course ground black pepper
3 tablespoons butter
1 tablespoon olive oil
2 ounces California brandy

Salt both sides of the steak pressing the salt into the flesh. Sprinkle both sides of the steak with the pepper and press into the steak. In a large skillet, heat the butter and oil and sauté the steak from 5 to 7 minutes on each side, depending upon the degree of rareness desired. Remove the steak to a warm platter. Add brandy to the pan, heat and pour over the steak. Serves 4.

Steak with green peppercorns

A few years ago, chefs began to accent the use of various peppercorns. Not content with black and white peppercorns, they began to present food dishes with green peppercorns and, later, pink peppercorns. This next recipe calls for the use of green peppercorns, but there is no reason you can't use whatever peppercorns you have in the kithcen.

3-pound sirloin steak, cut 1-1/2 inches thick
Salt
1 tablespoon California brandy
1 tablespoon green peppercorns, drained and crushed
1/4 cup heavy (whipping) cream
1/2 teaspoon Dijon mustard

Cut a piece of fat from the steak and render it in a sauté pan. Pan fry the steak to the desired degree of doneness. Transfer the steak to a warm platter and season with salt. Remove the fat from the pan. Add remaining ingredients, heat to the boil and pour the sauce over the steaks. Serves 3-4.

The heritage of California brandy can be traced back to men of diverse backgrounds and ethnic groups. In 1881, Robert Barton, a native of England who had been prominent in California earlier as a mining engineer, started a vineyard near Fresno. By 1883, he was busily advertising his establishment as the "greatest of all the Fresno vineyards."

Pepper steak mignonette

As you can see from the previous recipe, the chef leaves plenty of room to move about the culinary spectrum as he or she sees fit. As a chef, you could use six small steaks, no oil or, better yet, cook them in either clarified butter or grapeseed oil, flame the brandy before pouring the sauce over the steak, or add shallots, red or port wine, heavy cream, Dijon mustard or Madeira—the list is almost endless.

So here are some other innovations as served in the dining rooms of some of the great restaurants in the world.

6 steaks, one inch thick
1-1/2 tablespoons white pepper, coarsely cracked
3 tablespoons oil
3 tablespoons butter
1/4 cup California brandy
1/4 cup veal stock or red wine
2 tablespoons cold sweet butter

Press the pepper into the steak with the heel of your hand and let the steaks rest 30 minutes. Heat the oil and butter in a large sauté pan and cook the steaks to the desired degree of doneness. Remove the steaks to a warm platter. Turn up the heat and add the brandy. Swirl the liquid in the pan until it is reduced and slightly thick. Add stock or wine, blend the mixture well and add the butter. When the butter has melted, pour the sauce over the steaks. Serves 6.

Butterfly steak

Here is a different way of fixing steak. It can be grilled outdoors and then finished inside in a chafing dish at the table.

10-ounce sirloin, split and opened like a butterfly's wings
Salt and black pepper to taste
1 teaspoon Dijon mustard
1 teaspoon Worcestershire sauce
Dash of A-1 sauce (optional)
3 tablespoons beef stock
3 tablespoons California brandy

Grill the steak as you like it. Transfer the steak to a chafing dish. Add remaining ingredients except the brandy. Simmer until the juices are bubbling. Heat brandy to the sizzle, ignite and pour over steak. Serves 1-2.

Chocolate beef stew

Although John Sutter's first attempt at distilling brandy was unsuccessful, he might have eventually become one of California's premier brandy makers. In 1849, while Sutter was busy chasing gold-hungry miners off his property, his bumbling son sold his still to General Vallejo. Sutter was furious when he discovered what had happened, though Vallejo was delighted with his purchase.

Chocolate? Added to pot roast? I could hardly believe my ears.

My friend Juan and I were sitting under a 100-year-old olive tree. Siesta time was over and the bells of the Church of Santa Maria were gently reminding the ranch hands to return to work. Juan and I had spent the entire siesta talking about food and wine.

"Don't look as if you had just seen a giant lizard," he said. "The chocolate gives a winey taste to the stew, a trick my ancestors learned from the Aztecs. Besides, it is just a little bit of chocolate."

That night, Juan took me into his kitchen. Walking over to one of the stoves where a large black cast iron pot held tonight's delight, he gently lifted the cover and the smell of wine and spices filled my nose.

"Where is the chocolate?" I asked.

"Oh, that's only added at the last moment," he said.

Here is his recipe, just as he gave it to me.

3 pounds of pot roast, cut into cubes
3 tablespoons olive oil
1 large onion, chopped fine
3 cloves garlic, chopped fine
1 teaspoon salt
1 tablespoon flour
2 bay leaves
1 cup dry white wine
1/2 cup beef stock
1/3 cup water
1/4 cup California brandy
1 tablespoon white wine vinegar
1 tablespoon bitter chocolate, grated

In a deep kettle, braise the meat in the oil. Add the onion and garlic and cook until the onions are soft. Add salt and flour, stirring to mix well. Add remaining ingredients, except the chocolate. Cover tightly and simmer for 2 hours, or until the meat is done. Remove meat to warm platter. Skim fat from the sauce. Add chocolate and whisk until mixed. Strain. Serve the sauce separately. Serves 6.

Roast pork

One of my favorite dishes is roast pork. Here is a recipe that marries cider and brandy with a loin of pork.

8-pound loin of pork
Salt and fresh ground pepper to taste
8 baking apples, cored
8 large white onions
1-1/2 cups cider
2 tablespoons flour
1/4 cup California brandy

Generously salt and pepper the roast. Put the loin on a rack in a roasting pan and roast at 375 degrees for 1-1/2 hours. Pour off the fat. Surround the roast with the apples and onions, alternating them in the pan. Add 1 cup of the cider and roast another hour. When the pork is done, remove it to a warm platter. Surround the roast with the apples and onions. Skim fat from the pan juices. Stir in flour and cook over low heat. Add remaining cider and all the brandy. Stir, scraping the bottom so as to get all the brown particles which add flavor to the sauce. Simmer for 5 minutes. Serve sauce in a separate dish. Serves 8.

Brandied beef casserole

If your family likes casserole dishes and Mom only has a short time to cook in the kitchen, feast your eyes on this.

2 pounds stew meat
1 teaspoon garlic salt
1 teaspoon paprika
1/2 teaspoon basil
1/4 teaspoon thyme
2 tablespoons flour
2 tablespoons oil
1 large onion, cut into wedges
1/4 cup California brandy
10-1/2-ounce can beef broth
2 cups mushrooms, sliced

Toss the meat in a mixture made from the salt, paprika, basil, thyme and flour. Heat the oil in a deep skillet and when hot, brown the meat all over. Add onions, brandy and stock to the pot. Cover and cook 1 to 1-1/2 hours or until the meat is tender. Add mushrooms last 5 minutes of cooking. Serves 4.

Veal savoyarde

This is an unusual dish. I first tasted it in the south of France at a little nondescript restaurant that most people would ignore. Its facade was plain, just as plain as its interior. I sat down and the chef/owner told me that he had fresh veal on the menu today, a dish prepared in the style of the province of Savoy.

I nodded my head, ordered a bottle of white wine and waited. Fifteen minutes later, he brought out the veal dish and it was excellent. I didn't need the recipe, for it was easy to duplicate.

12 thin slices of veal scallops
6 slices Gruyere cheese
6 slices cooked ham
Dijon mustard
2 eggs
2 tablespoons oil
2 tablespoons water
2 cups fresh bread crumbs
3 tablespoons butter
3 tablespoons olive oil
1/4 cup California brandy
2 tablespoons sour cream

Make six sandwiches of the veal scallops, cheese and ham, by putting a slice of cheese and ham between two veal scallops and pressing the edges together. Brush them with the mustard. Mix the egg, oil and water together. Dip the veal sandwiches into the egg and then bread crumbs. Sauté the scallops in the butter and oil until they are done and set aside. Deglaze the pan with the brandy and when it sizzles, flame it. Add the sour cream and mix well. Pour the sauce on a heated platter. Place veal on top of sauce. Serves 6.

Tournedos a ma facon

Tournedos is the best cut of beef you will ever taste. It was a French chef, Auguste Escoffier, who elevated that little piece of beef to exalted heights, when he created Tournedos Rossini, for the great Italian composer Gioacchino Rossini.

To prepare his dish, Escoffier sautéed some two-inch-thick tournedos in butter and arranged them in the form of a crown on fried bread slices. On each tournedo, he set a slice of foie gras that had been seasoned and fried in butter. Then he placed a thick slice of black truffle on top of the foie gras and covered his creation with a Madeira-flavored brown sauce.

Today we are all eating lighter, so I have developed a lighter version of the heavy Escoffier dish, which fits into today's lifestyle.

1 tournedo, about 4-5 ounces
2 tablespoons clarified butter
1/4 cup California brandy
1/2 cup beef stock
1/4 cup Madeira
1 tablespoon cornstarch
Salt and pepper to taste

Sauté the tournedo in the butter to the desired degree of doneness. Remove the meat to a warm platter. Deglaze the pan with the brandy and ignite. Add stock and reduce to almost a glaze. Mix Madeira and cornstarch to a smooth paste. Add to the mixture. Salt and pepper to taste. Pour sauce over steak. Serves 1.

Westpoint graduate and Civil War veteran, General Henry M. Naglee was one of the most famous California brandy makers in the 1870s. His brandy and romantic pursuits were widely acclaimed. He was the subject of a sensational book, "THE LOVE LIFE OF GENERAL NAGLEE" which was complete with love letters written by him and a drawing of the general in his bath tub full of brandy.

$\mathcal{S}$teak in chemise

No chef likes to be outdone by his competitor. Most chefs spend many hours dreaming about and creating new dishes. Here is an unknown chef's creation, and a good one too.

6 large crepes
6 small steaks, filets or sirloins
2 tablespoons black pepper, crushed
Salt
1/4 cup butter
1/4 cup oil
1/2 cup white wine
3/4 cup heavy (whipping) cream
3 tablespoons California brandy

Press the pepper into the steaks with the heel of your hand. Salt the steaks. In a large skillet, melt the butter, add the oil and sear the steaks on both sides. Cook them 3-4 minutes, depending upon the degree of desired doneness. Remove steaks to a warm platter and partially wrap each in a crepe. Discard all but a tablespoon of the oil in the pan and add the cream and brandy. Cook until the sauce has reduced and becomes slightly thick. Pour the sauce over the steaks. Put under the broiler for 1 minute. Serves 6.

$\mathcal{S}wedish\ roast$

Here is a Swedish way of cooking beef. It is a boon to the harried cook.

4 pounds eye of the round
1/4 cup butter
1 tablespoon clarified butter or olive oil
2 cups onions, diced
1/2 cup carrots, sliced thin
1/4 cup California brandy
2 cups boiling water
1/4 teaspoon allspice
2 bay leaves, broken in half
1 tablespoon red wine vinegar
2 tablespoons instant flour
1-1/2 cup heavy (whipping) cream

In a large pan, heat the oil and butter, then add the onions, carrots and meat. Sear the meat all over and add remaining ingredients except the flour and cream. Cover and simmer for 2 hours or until the meat is tender. When the meat is cooked, remove to a warm platter. Mix the flour and cream to a smooth paste and add to the juices. Cook 2-3 minutes to thicken the sauce. Serve sauce separately. Serves 6.

$\mathcal{S}imple\ beef\ stew$

If you are still in the mood for simple dishes, here is one I whipped up some 10 years ago. It just about makes itself.

1 one-inch-thick slice of pot roast
3 carrots, peeled and halved
3 onions, peeled and quartered
3 potatoes, peeled and halved
1 small turnip
1 bottle of red wine
1/2 cup California brandy
Salt and black pepper to taste

Trim the meat of any fat. Lay the meat in the bottom of a large pan or kettle. Add remaining ingredients and simmer for 35-45 minutes, or until the vegetables are tender. Lift the meat and vegetables from the pot onto a warm platter. Taste and correct the sauce. If you want a thicker sauce, mix 1 tablespoon of cold water with 1 tablespoon of cornstarch and stir it into the mixture. Serves 6.

Filet angelique

Another simple way to prepare beef and brandy!

6 filets, about 1 inch thick
Clove of garlic
4 ounces butter
Salt and pepper to taste
4 tablespoons California brandy

Rub the steaks with the salt and pepper and the cut side of a clove of garlic. Melt half the butter in a skillet and sauté the steaks until they are brown on both sides. Add remaining butter. Heat brandy and flame. Pour over steaks. Serves 6.

Filet of beef flambé

THE RIGHT OF WAY

Every so often you have to splurge. So go ahead, get yourself a filet of beef, invite a few friends over and open that bottle of Cabernet Sauvignon you have been saving.

5- or 6-pound filet of beef
4 tablespoons olive oil
1 teaspoon fresh ground black pepper
Salt
1/3 cup California brandy
3 tablespoons butter
1 tablespoon parsley, minced

Rub the filet with the oil and pepper. Place the filet on a rack in a roasting pan and roast at 450 degrees for 35 minutes. When done, salt the roast and let it rest for 10 minutes. Just before carving, heat the brandy to the sizzle, ignite and pour it over the roast. Add the butter and top with parsley. Serves 6.

Veal scallopine flambé

Veal is appearing on more and more menus in American homes than at any other time in our history. It is a meat that people are taking to and serving at special dinners. Good veal is not hard to find and can be served in a variety of ways.

12 veal scallopine, pounded very thin
3 tablespoons butter
3 tablespoons olive oil
Salt and white pepper to taste
3 tablespoons California brandy
3 tablespoons white wine
1 tablespoon cold water
1 tablespoon cornstarch
1-1/4 cups heavy (whipping) cream

Sauté the scallopine in the butter and oil over high heat. Salt and pepper to taste and cook 3 more minutes. Heat the brandy to the sizzle, ignite it and pour over the scallopine. Transfer the scallopine to a warm platter. To the pan juices, add the wine and deglaze the pan. Mix the water and cornstarch into a smooth paste, add it to the cream and pour the mixture into the pan. Cook until the sauce becomes slightly thick. Check seasonings. Pour sauce over veal. Serves 6.

Scallopine a la creme

General Henry M. Naglee of San Jose, California developed an international reputation as a California Brandy maker in the 1870s. His famed "Burgundy" Brandy, made from Pinot Noir grapes amazed the French and received a rating of "100" on a scale of 1 to 100 at international competitions. His "Reisling" Brandy was likewise acclaimed, scoring an "85".

Again, the simple dishes are what people like. Here is a veal, brandy and cream recipe that anyone can make and be proud to serve their friends.

12 veal scallopine
4 tablespoons butter
1/4 cup California brandy
1 cup heavy (whipping) cream

Sauté the scallopine in the butter. Put the scallopine on a warm platter and keep warm. Add the brandy to the skillet, heat to the sizzle and flame. Scrape the particles from the skillet. Add the cream and reduce until slightly thick. Pour sauce over veal. Serves 6.

Veal steak diane savini

Angelo Pozzi of Savini restaurant in Milan likes to prepare this special veal dish in a chafing dish at his customer's table.

1-pound veal steak, pounded very thin
1 teaspoon dry English mustard
1 teaspoon water
2 tablespoons Dijon mustard
1 tablespoon olive oil
6 tablespoons butter
Salt and white pepper to taste
6 tablespoons California brandy
3 tablespoons chives, chopped
1 teaspoon Worcestershire sauce

Make a paste of the dry mustard, water and Dijon mustard. Coat the veal with the mixture and brush it with the olive oil. In a skillet, sauté the veal in half the butter for 3 minutes on each side until brown. Transfer the veal to a hot platter, and sprinkle it with salt and pepper. Heat the brandy to the sizzle, ignite and pour into the pan. When the flame dies out, add remaining ingredients. Bring to the boil. Pour sauce over veal. Serves 3.

Spareribs marinade

Pork has long been a favorite American dish. It was and still is one of the best meats that produces a rich, dark and toothsome gravy. If you like pork spareribs over the charcoal grill, here is a marinade that you will find hard to top.

4-5 pounds spareribs
1 cup California brandy
1 cup red wine
1 cup tomato purée
1 tablespoon salt
1/2 tablespoon fresh ground black pepper
3 cloves garlic, crushed

Marinate the ribs in the sauce for at least 12 hours. Drain the ribs. Put the marinade in a saucepan and reduce it by half its original volume. Put the ribs on the charcoal grill and cook until done, basting them every 10 minutes with the reduced marinade. Serves 6.

Saddle of lamb jeanette

A saddle of lamb is a splendid thing. It not only looks regal but it tastes kingly, especially if prepared using the recipe below.

8-pound saddle of lamb
1 cup California brandy
1/4 cup olive oil
1 bay leaf
4 cloves
1/2 clove garlic, crushed
1/4 cup onions, minced
2 sprigs of mint
Pinch of ground cinnamon
Salt and pepper to taste
1 cup sherry
2 tablespoons flour
2 tablespoons parsley, minced

In 1863, Kohler & Frohling, brandy makers in Los Angeles, exported their product to New York and Boston and even issued a catalog with the headline: "Let Americans Support American Industry". California brandy makers might use the same phrase today.

Make a marinade of half the brandy and all of the olive oil, bay leaf, cloves, garlic, onions, mint, cinnamon, salt and pepper. Marinate the saddle at least 3 hours, turning it every half hour. Transfer the saddle and marinade to a roasting pan and roast at 450 degrees to 20 minutes. Lower the temperature to 350 degrees and roast until the lamb is rare, about 20 minutes per pound. Remove the saddle from the pan to a warm serving platter. Heat the remaining 1/2 cup of brandy to the sizzle. Ignite it and pour it over the saddle. Skim the fat from the pan juices. Add the sherry and flour and simmer for 5 minutes. Taste and adjust the seasonings. Strain the sauce into a sauceboat. Serves 6.

Paupiettes hébert

No one knows exactly why they are called "birds". They don't fly; they have no feathers and they don't lay eggs. The French call them "little birds without heads." However, they are better known in the world of cuisine as "paupiettes."

12 slices veal scallopine
12 slices prosciutto, sliced paper thin
12 pieces Mozzarella cheese, 1 inch long, 1/4 inch wide
3 tablespoons olive oil
1/4 cup California brandy
3 tablespoons Madeira wine
3 tablespoons chicken stock
3 tablespoons sour cream
Salt and pepper to taste

Take one veal scallopine and place one slice of prosciutto on it. On top of the prosciutto, place one slice of the cheese. Roll the scallopine up, tucking in the sides. Tie with string. Repeat this 11 more times until all the scallopine are rolled and tied. Sauté the birds in the oil until cooked and brown all over. Remove to a warm platter. Deglaze the pan with the brandy and when it sizzles, flame it. Add the Madeira and stock and reduce by half. Add sour cream and let it thicken for 1 minute. Pour the sauce over the birds. Serves 4.

Lamb steak rachel

Lamb was first served in the Middle East and gradually made its way across the ocean to the New World. Today, lamb is a part of the American diet. I like lamb in many forms. Here are two of my favorites.

2 lamb chops 3/4 inch thick
2 tablespoons butter
1 tablespoon shallots, minced
1 tablespoon chives, chopped
1 tablespoon parsley, chopped
1 tablespoon Worcestershire sauce
Salt and pepper to taste
1/4 cup California brandy

Sauté the chops in half the butter over high heat for 2 minutes on each side. Remove the steaks and add the shallots to the pan. Sauté them until they are soft and return the steaks to the pan. Add chives, parsley, sauce, remaining butter, and salt and pepper. Cook 1 more minute. Heat the brandy to the sizzle, ignite and pour over the steaks. Serves 2.

Chapter six
Brandy &
Seafood

America is having a love affair with seafood. More of it is consumed today and more and more seafood stores are being established in the towns and villages throughout the United States.

The seafood craze is a healthy one because seafood is recommended by doctors as a way to help control your weight and remain healthy. And America is health conscious.

It has always been amazing to me how well seafood and brandy go together. Whether it is shrimp, lobsters, crayfish, crabs, trout, sole, snapper, salmon, scallops, mussels, pike, oysters, or halibut, brandy is ready and willing to help make seafood dishes taste better. And one seafood that takes to the addition of brandy in its preparation is shrimp.

Shrimp have been caught as close as a mile off the shore and as deep as 1,800 feet off the edge of the continental shelf. They are classified in the United States by how many make up a pound. Some fish markets will advertise shrimp by using these numbers. The higher the number, the more shrimp per pound and that means the smaller the shrimp.

The shrimp is a hardy crustacean. The female lays about 1,000,000 eggs, which hatch after 12 hours. The shrimp goes through a dozen molts (a shedding of its skin) before it becomes the shrimp we eat. Because the shrimp is delicate, it should never be overcooked. Once in a while you can get fresh shrimp and I urge you to buy them whenever possible, since they taste a hundred times better than frozen shrimp.

Scampi lucullus

Lucullus was an early apostle of the gourmet life. He once instructed his chef to spend $1,000 per person, per meal. One day, after a very hard day in the Roman Senate, Lucullus came home to dine and found that his chef had not spent the $1,000 for his meal. Asking the chef why he had failed, the chef explained it away with, "But, Master, you are dining alone ..."

Lucullus exploded. "That is precisely why dinner is to be extra special. Lucullus is the guest of Lucullus."

I don't know how many times you have been your own guest at dinner, but when your friends taste this shrimp dish, you will never be alone again.

1/2 cup onions, minced
1/4 cup butter, plus 2 tablespoons
1-1/2 pounds mushrooms, sliced
36 raw shrimp, shelled and deveined
1/2 cup mango chutney or your favorite chutney
1/4 cup California brandy
1 cup heavy (whipping) cream
Cayenne to taste
Salt and pepper to taste

In a large sauté pan, sauté the onions in the 2 tablespoons of butter. Add remaining butter and sauté the mushrooms until browned. With a slotted spoon, transfer the onions and mushrooms to a dish. In the same pan, sauté the shrimp for 30 seconds. Transfer the shrimp to the mushroom and onion dish. Add to the pan the chutney and brandy and cook the mixture over high heat until the brandy has evaporated. Stir in the cream, bring the liquid to the boil and simmer until the mixture thickens. Add mushrooms, onions and shrimp and cook another 3-4 minutes. Season the sauce with cayenne, salt and pepper. Serves 4-6.

God, in His greatness, sent the grapes
To cheer both great and small;
Little fools will drink too much,
And great fools, none at all.
—ANONYMOUS

Brandied shrimp with cream

If you are looking for an elegant dish to serve as a main course, I would suggest this next recipe. I once served it as a main dish and so help me, my guests ate every drop of it at the expense of the vegetables, bread, butter, etc. The next time I served this dish, I doubled the recipe, forsook the vegetables and served just a salad.

2-1/2 pounds raw shrimp, shelled and deveined
5 tablespoons butter
Salt and pepper to taste
Nutmeg to taste
3/4 cup California brandy
4 egg yolks
3/4 cup heavy (whipping) cream

Lay the shrimp on a board. Split them down the backs without cutting all the way through. Melt the butter in a saucepan and sauté the shrimp until they turn pink. Season them with salt, pepper and nutmeg. Heat the brandy in a pan to the sizzle. Ignite the spirit and pour it over the shrimp. Tilt the pan back and forth until the flame dies out. Simmer the shrimp for 5 minutes. Remove from the heat. Beat together the yolks with the cream and gradually stir the mixture into the pan juices. Serves 6.

Scampi alla venezia

Harry's Bar in Venice, is a star-studded hangout for the rich and famous. His place was made famous by "Papa" Hemingway, who patronized the bar and used it as a meeting place for all his friends. Not too far from Harry's Bar are several restaurants that specialized in this next dish.

5 tablespoons butter
2 pounds raw shrimp, shelled and deveined
3 tablespoons California brandy
1/2 cup tomatoes, peeled, seeded and chopped
1 cup heavy (whipping) cream
Salt and white pepper to taste

Melt the butter in a skillet and sauté the shrimp for 2 minutes. Heat the brandy to the sizzle, flame and pour over the shrimp. Add remaining ingredients and cook over low heat for 8 minutes. Correct seasonings. Serves 6.

Shrimp, lake como style

Here's another Italian presentation of shrimp. This one comes from the Lake Como area, one of the most beautiful resorts in the world.

3 tablespoons olive oil
3 tablespoons butter
1/4 cup onion, minced
2 tablespoons carrot, grated
1 bay leaf, crushed
1-1/2 pounds raw shrimp, shelled and deveined
1/3 cup California brandy
1 cup tomatoes, peeled, seeded and chopped
Salt and pepper to taste
1 tablespoon lemon juice
1 teaspoon flour
3/4 cup heavy (whipping) cream

Heat the oil and 2 tablespoons butter in a sauté pan and cook onion, carrot and bay leaf for 10 minutes. Add shrimp and cook another 3 minutes. Heat the brandy to the sizzle, ignite and pour over the shrimp. Add tomatoes, salt, pepper and lemon juice. Simmer for 7-8 minutes. Remove shrimp to warm platter. Cook sauce over high heat for a few minutes. Cream the flour with the remaining butter and add it to the sauce along with the cream. Cook over low heat for several minutes making sure the sauce is smooth. Pour over shrimp. Serves 6.

Most California brandy is rectified, or blended with other brandies. Each brandymaster has his own special master formula, one of the most closely guarded secrets in the world of brandy. If Macy's doesn't tell Gimbels . . . . .?

Skewered shrimp & brandy mayonnaise

Skewered shrimp, either broiled indoors or outdoors should be served with a special Brandy Mayonnaise.

24 raw shrimp, shelled and deveined
1 cup California brandy
1/4 cup tarragon vinegar
8 slices of bacon, cut in thirds
Brandy Mayonnaise (see recipe below)

Mix half the brandy and all the tarragon vinegar together in a shallow dish and let the shrimp marinate in them at least 3 hours. Wrap each shrimp in 1/3 slice of bacon. Thread them on skewers and broil 3 inches from the heat for 6 minutes, or until the bacon is crisp. Put the skewers in a chafing dish. Heat the remaining 1/2 cup of brandy to the sizzle and ignite. Pour the flaming spirit over the skewers. Serve with Brandy Mayonnaise. Serves 6.

BRANDY MAYONNAISE

1 cup mayonnaise, homemade if possible
1 tablespoon California brandy

Whisk the brandy into the mayonnaise with a wire whisk. Makes 1 cup.

Mussels victoria

This mussel dish makes an excellent spring luncheon dish or it can be served as a fish course in a more elaborate meal.

4 tablespoons butter
4 tablespoons parsley, minced
2 cloves garlic, minced
2 cups chicken stock
1/2 cup white wine
1/2 cup California brandy
3 dozen mussels

In the butter sauté the parsley, onions and garlic for 2 minutes. Add stock, wine and brandy. Cook 1 more minute. Add mussels and cover. Steam until the shells open, about 5 minutes. Discard any mussels that do not open. Serves 4.

Mussels in cardinal sauce

Mussels are available throughout the United States. Some states have them six to eight months during the year while others have them only a few months. Nevertheless, mussels are excellent either as a first course or a main entrée, especially with French bread, a white wine and a small salad.

Mussels should be trimmed of their beards. You can do this simply by pulling the beard away from the shell using a sharp knife. Mussels sometimes have sand and grit inside their shells. To rid them of this sand and grit, put the mussels in water, preferably sea water, and throw in several handfuls of flour. The mussels will gorge themselves on the flour and get rid of the sand and grit.

The first time I tasted mussels, I immediately named them one of my favorite shellfish. I have been hooked on them ever since.

5 dozen mussels
1-1/2 cup water
1 cup white wine
3 tablespoons tomato paste
2 tablespoons lemon juice
1 tablespoon sherry
1 tablespoon California brandy
1 clove garlic, minced
1/2 cup onions, minced
2 cups mayonnaise
1-1/2 tablespoons sour cream
1 teaspoon horseradish
Salt to taste
Paprika to taste

Steam the mussels in 1 cup water and all the white wine in a covered kettle or pot until the shells open. Discard the top shells. Make a sauce by cooking the tomato paste, lemon juice, sherry, brandy, garlic, onions and remaining 1/2 cup water in a saucepan until the mixture has been reduced to one-third its original volume. Strain the sauce and let it cool. Add remaining ingredients. Chill the sauce for 2 hours. Top each mussel with a small amount of the sauce. Serves 8.

Lobster has always been associated with such epicurean delights as cavier and vintage champagne. I don't think that is valid today. Just a week ago some friends came to visit us from Boston and they brought with them 12 live lobsters packed in seaweed. The price averaged out at $5.50 per lobster, which is three to five dollars cheaper than I can get the same lobsters in California.

When the Pilgrims first landed in the United States they faced the awesome task of cooking the gargantuan lobsters they caught: huge monsters five to six feet in length. They have long since disappeared from our shores and today lobster buffs prefer the ones weighing one to one-and-a-half pounds; claiming that the bigger lobsters are tougher.

The lobster, like the crawfish and crab, is a cannibal. To the lobster, a choice meal is another lobster. Nevertheless, the lobster is one of nature's great creations and one of the best shellfish you will ever taste.

Here are a few hints when dealing with lobsters.

● *To kill a live lobster instantly, plunge a knife into the lobster where the body and the tail section meet. This severs the spinal cord.*

● *Avoid if possible cooked lobsters you see in the fish market. You are better off buying the raw frozen lobster tails because they will taste better after you have cooked them than pre-cooked lobsters.*

● *Don't overlook the meat in the head of the lobster. I always pick out the meat from the head of the lobster and make a lobster salad or lobster bisque. Too many people think that the tail and the claws are the only meat from a lobster.*

One of California's oldest wineries, Almaden, is also the state's oldest existing brandy distillery. The October 8, 1868 edition of the San Jose Weekly Mercury mentions that Charles LeFranc, Almaden's founder, won a prize for "the finest grape brandy entered in the Santa Clara County Fair."

Lobster cocktail with brandy

If you like picnics, and want to impress your friends, here is a special lobster cocktail mix that you can whip out as a first course. And if you don't like picnics, just serve it at your next dinner party and still surprise your friends.

2 cups lobster meat, cut in bite-size pieces
1/2 cup mayonnaise
1 tablespoon tomato catsup
2 tablespoons lemon juice
1 tablespoon parsley, minced
2 tablespoons chives, minced
Salt and pepper to taste
2 tablespoons California brandy

Mix the lobster meat and mayonnaise in a bowl and refrigerate for 1 hour. Add remaining ingredients. Mix well. Chill for 2 hours. For picnics, pack the mixture in small individual containers. Serves 6.

Lobster in brandy cream sauce

This recipe is from Craig Claiborne's weekly food column in the Sunday magazine section of the *New York Times*. I have not always agreed with Mr. Claiborne's palate; and as he recently wrote, likes and dislikes about food are for the most part subjective. I agree, and I also agree on this lobster dish. The only change I have made is to use California brandy, which I think makes the lobster taste better. Yes, it is subjective.

4 live lobsters, about 1-1/4 pounds each
1/4 cup olive oil
3 tablespoons shallots or green onions, finely chopped
3 tablespoons onions, finely chopped
1 tablespoon garlic, minced
2 tablespoons California brandy
1-1/2 cups tomatoes, chopped, fresh or canned
1/2 teaspoon dried thyme
1 cup dry white wine
1 tablespoon parsley, chopped
Salt and pepper to taste
1 cup heavy (whipping) cream

Plunge a knife into each lobster where the body and tail section meet to sever the spinal cord. This will kill the lobster instantly. Break off the tail and set aside in a large bowl. Break off the claws and add to the large bowl. Cut off the small feeler claws and add to the bowl. Discard the tough sac near the eyes. Split the carcass in half widthwise. Heat the oil in a deep, heavy skillet large enough to hold the lobsters. When the oil starts to smoke, add the lobster pieces. Cook, stirring, about 5 minutes. Add shallots, onion and garlic. Sprinkle in brandy. Add tomatoes, thyme, wine, parsley, salt and pepper. Cook stirring over high heat for 1 minute. Cover and cook another 15 minutes. Remove the tails and claws from the skillet and let them cool briefly. Continue to cook the remainder of the ingredients and add the cream. Cook, uncovered, over high heat about 10 minutes to reduce the sauce. Meanwhile, when the tails and claws are cool enough to handle, break or crack the claws and tails. Remove the meat. Add meat to the sauce along with accumulated juices. Serve the lobster pieces in the sauce and serve with fluffy rice or buttered noodles. Serves 6-8.

Lobster piccante

Grapes for brandymaking were grown only in vineyards scattered throughout the San Joaquin Valley until Francis Eisen, a native of Germany, settled in Fresno. In 1873, Eisen set out the first commercial vineyards in the Valley. A contemporary reported that "so fruitless was the first effort considered by the residents of the county, that individuals frequently remarked that they would be able to eat the entire vintage."

No amateur, Eisen persisted with his vision of producing fine wine and brandy, and the 1875 vintage proved him right. By 1881 he was cultivating 200 acres of vineyards and was gaining a good reputation for his brandy.

Lobster tails have been popular for more than 25 years, ever since South African Rock Lobster tails were introduced. These little frozen morsels can be substituted for live lobsters, especially if live lobsters are too expensive. I have used these tails many times and have never been disappointed.

4 lobster tails, thawed
1/3 cup butter
1/3 cup olive oil
1/3 cup onions, minced
1 clove garlic, minced
1/4 cup California brandy
1/4 cup gin
1/2 cup white wine
2 cups heavy (whipping) cream
2 teaspoons salt
1/2 teaspoon fresh grated white pepper
1 tablespoon fresh lemon juice

Cut each lobster tail into four pieces. Heat the butter and oil in a deep skillet and sauté the tails over high heat until they turn red. Pour off the fat. Add onions, garlic, brandy and gin. Cook until all the liquid has been evaporated. Watch the pan carefully so that the mixture doesn't burn. Add wine and cook until no liquid remains. Add cream, salt and pepper. cover and simmer for 15 minutes. Remove the meat and place on a warm serving platter. Add lemon juice to the sauce and reduce to about 1 cup. Pour sauce over lobster. Serves 2-4.

Lobster americaine

Lobster Americaine has long been debated as to whether it was named after America, was created by a French chef who loved America, or any other story you would care to invent. Actually, no one really knows the origin. And I think most people don't really care. It's the dish that counts.

3 live lobsters, 1-1/2 pounds each
1/4 cup olive oil
Salt and black pepper to taste
3 tablespoons butter
1/2 cup onions, chopped
1 carrot, grated
1/4 cup California brandy
1 bay leaf
1/2 cup canned tomato sauce
2 tomatoes, peeled, seeded and chopped
3/4 cup white wine
1 clove garlic, minced
1/2 teaspoon cayenne

Plunge a knife into each lobster where the body and tail section meet to sever the spinal cord. This will kill the lobster instantly. Remove the claws and crack them. Chop the tails into 4 pieces. Heat the oil in a large skillet, salt and pepper the lobster pieces and sauté them for 5 minutes or until they turn red. In a deep casserole, melt 2 tablespoons butter and sauté the onions and carrots until brown. Add lobster pieces. Heat brandy to the sizzle, ignite and pour the flaming spirit over the lobster pieces. Add bay leaf, tomato sauce, tomatoes, wine, garlic and cayenne. Cover and simmer for 20 minutes. Serves 6.

FOUR DOLLARS PER GALLON was the price of California Brandy shipped up the coast by Jean Luis Vignes in 1840 and sold in Monterey and San Francisco. Interesting, the Brandy traveled on a ship named "Mooson".

Lobster tarts

"We are having lobsters for lunch," the note read. How could I turn it down. I went, I ate and I got the recipe from my charming hostess.

2 cups cooked lobster meat, chopped
2 tablespoons butter
1 tablespoon onion, chopped
1 tablespoon parsley, minced
1/4 cup California brandy
1/2 cup heavy (whipping) cream
2 egg yolks
6 medium tart shells
Grated Parmesan cheese
Buttered bread crumbs

Sauté the chopped lobster meat in butter, onions and parsley, until the onions are transparent. Add the brandy. Heat the cream to warm and mix in yolks. Add to mixture. Divide the mixture into 6 equal portions and fill the tarts with the portions. Sprinkle the cheese and crumbs on top. Place under the broiler and brown. Serves 6.

The majority of California brandy made today is distilled from the juice of the Thompson Seedless grape that was introduced to the San Joaquin Valley in 1872 by an Englishman named William Thompson. The variety soon gained popularity and Thompson was promptly dubbed "Seedless Thompson" although he fathered 17 children.

ome people call them crayfish, some crawfish, some mudbugs and the French call them "écrevisses." No matter what you call them, no one knows more about crayfish than the Cajuns and Creoles of Louisiana. In fact Breaux Bridge, Louisiana, is called the "Crawfish Capital Of The World." Louisiana is said to produce 99 percent of the U.S. crawfish harvest, although there are small crawfish farms springing up all over the United States. Tons of crawfish are taken from the Sacramento, California, area every year. Crawfish business ventures are said to be forming in Wisconsin, Minnesota and various other states.

Even though there seems to be an interest in crawfish, no region of the United States has a bigger "cult of the crawfish" than the people of Southern Louisiana. Not only do they just plain boil the crawfish, they make pies, bisques, etouffes, jambalayas, croquettes, gumbos—the list seems endless.

An old Cajun once told me how he ate crawfish. "You squeezes de tail an' sucks de haid."

Cajun boiled crawfish

The people of southern Louisiana love their crawfish just boiled. I don't know where this recipe comes from but it is one of the best court bouillons I know of to bring out the best of any crawfish.

1 gallon of water
1/2 cup California brandy
1/2 cup white wine
1 onion, thinly sliced
1 clove garlic, crushed
1/2 teaspoon cayenne
1 sprig thyme
1 rib of celery
12 allspice berries
3 bay leaves
6 whole cloves
1/2 cup salt
4 dozen live crawfish
2 lemons

In a large kettle combine the first 12 ingredients. Bring to the boil and simmer for 30 minutes. Add crawfish and lemons and boil for 15-20 minutes. Let the crawfish cool before eating them. Serves 6.

Crawfish bordelaise

Anything cooked "a la Bordelaise" can mean any number of treatments to a dish. To one chef it means with red wine and foie gras; to another it means with mushrooms; and to another it means in the style of Bordeaux, whatever that means. In this case, it means crawfish cooked with minced vegetables and flamed in California brandy.

2 tablespoons butter
1 carrot, minced
1 onion, minced
1 clove garlic, crushed
2 sprigs parsley
Pinch of dried thyme
1 bay leaf, crushed
4 tomatoes, peeled, seeded and chopped
1/2 teaspoon salt
4 dozen live crawfish
1/4 cup California brandy
2 cups white wine
3 tablespoons butter
1 tablespoon flour

Melt the butter in a saucepan and sauté the carrot, onion, garlic, parsley, thyme and bay leaf for 15 minutes or until they are soft. Add tomatoes, salt and crawfish and cook until the crawfish have turned red. Heat the brandy to the sizzle, ignite and pour the flaming spirit over the crawfish. When the flame has gone out, add the wine and cook another 12 minutes. Mix the flour and butter together. Remove the crawfish to a heated platter. Cook the remaining liquid until it is reduced by half. Add the butter/flour mixture to thicken the sauce. Taste and correct seasonings. Pour sauce over crawfish. Serves 6.

In 1878, the Reverend John I. Bleasdale of Australia participated in a formal tasting of California brandy at the Mechanic's Institute in San Francisco. Dr. Bleasdale, an analytical chemist and highly regarded wine expert, highly praised many of the Califorña brandys and subjected the best to chemical analysis. He found them to be: "chemically pure spirits, free from any admixture or adulteration whatever, free of dreadful fusel oil so abundant in ordinary liquors". He further stated: "I could easily recognize in these samples the distinctive bouquet of their respective wines, alongside of the brandy flavor proper, derived from the aromatic ethers formed during fermentation."

Crawfish cardinale

Because crawfish are so good to eat, my first recipe, considered to be the haute cuisine of all crawfish dishes, will set the stage for what is to come. Rima and Richard Collins in their excellent book, *The New Orleans Cookbook,* (Alfred Knopf) claim that this next dish was first introduced at Antoine's several decades ago by a talented French-speaking Cajun whose name is lost in the annals of time, but whose creation lives on. This recipe is from their book.

5 tablespoons salted butter
1/3 cup onion, finely chopped
1 tablespoon flour
1/4 cup heavy (whipping) cream
3/4 cup milk
1 cup crawfish tails, about 20 tails
3/4 teaspoon salt
1/4 teaspoon fresh ground white pepper
1/4 teaspoon cayenne
1/8 teaspoon mace
1/8 teaspoon allspice
1/8 teaspoon cloves
1 whole bay leaf, crushed
3 tablespoons California brandy
1 tablespoon dry white wine
1 tablespoon parsley, finely minced
1/4 teaspoon garlic, finely minced

In a small heavy skillet or sauté pan, melt 2 tablespoons of the butter over low heat. Add the onion and sauté until soft. In another heavy skillet or sauté pan, melt the remaining butter, add the flour and cook over low heat, stirring constantly, until a light yellow roux is formed. Turn off the heat and add the contents of the first skillet and slowly blend in cream and milk. Turn the heat on very low and cook until the mixture thickens, stirring constantly. Add crawfish tails and mix well. Stir in the salt, pepper, cayenne, mace, allspice, clove and bay leaf. Add brandy and white wine and simmer over low heat for 4 minutes, stirring all the time. Sprinkle in the parsley and garlic and simmer for 10 more minutes. Serve in heated individual ramekins or gratin dishes. Serves 4.

Scallops flamed with brandy

The scallop is a relative of the mussel, the oyster and the clam. Unlike them, he does not reside on sand or rock. He scoots about the ocean, zig-zagging forward when necessary and shooting backwards to elude a starfish or octopus. The scallop has fifty eyes to spot his predators and the only way he can be captured is by being dredged for by commercial fishing boats.

Scallops have been caught the size of a catcher's mitt, sometimes called "pie plates" by the scallop fishermen. In the United States, the scallops are taken from their shells by the fishermen on the boats. In Europe, people buy the whole shell and body, since like oysters and clams, every bit of the scallop is edible. The shells make useful baking dishes or bowls.

1-1/2 pounds sea scallops
1 teaspoon salt
Water
1 cup butter
2 tablespoons California brandy
Lemon wedges

Put the scallops in a saucepan with the salt and water to cover. Bring the water to the simmer and barely poach the scallops for 2-3 minutes, until they turn opaque. Drain the scallops. In a skillet melt the butter over high heat. Add the scallops and toss until the butter turns light brown. Heat the brandy to the sizzle, ignite and pour over scallops. When the flame dies out, serve the scallops with the lemon wedges. Serves 4.

An article published in an 1890 issue of the San Francisco Examiner described brandy distilled at the San Gabriel Wine Company in Southern California as "highly superior to the dubious beverage made in France."

Scallops roma

This scallop recipe marries scallops, tomatoes, thyme and California brandy for a different treat.

8 tablespoons butter
1 carrot, minced
1 onion, minced
2 shallots, minced
2 stalks parsley, minced
1 sprig thyme
1 bay leaf
2 pounds scallops
1 cup white wine
3 tomatoes, peeled, seeded and chopped
1/4 cup California brandy

In 4 tablespoons of butter, sauté the carrots, onions, shallots and parsley until they are lightly browned. Add thyme and bay leaf and cook another 15 minutes over low heat. Add scallops and cook until they are lightly browned. Add wine and tomatoes and simmer for 10 minutes. Heat the brandy to the sizzle, flame and pour into the mixture. Remove scallops. Keep warm. Add remaining butter and cook 2 more minutes. Pour sauce over scallops. Serves 6.

Brandy is called the "Soul of the Grape" because it is wine that has been distilled down to its essential elements.

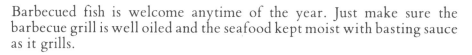

Barbecued halibut steaks

Barbecued fish is welcome anytime of the year. Just make sure the barbecue grill is well oiled and the seafood kept moist with basting sauce as it grills.

1/3 cup California brandy
1/3 cup fresh lemon juice
1/4 teaspoon dill weed
1 bay leaf
4 halibut steaks, about 1-1/2 pounds
1 medium red onion, sliced thin
1/2 lemon, sliced thin
1/3 cup chili sauce
2 tablespoons butter, melted
Salt

Combine the first four ingredients in a shallow bowl. Place the steaks in the bowl and top with the onion and lemon slices. Refrigerate for 1 hour. Drain steaks, reserving marinade. Place steaks over hot coals. Combine chili sauce and butter with reserved marinade. Baste the steaks every 3 minutes with the mixture. Cook the steaks about 5 minutes on each side. Sprinkle with salt. Serves 4.

Greek baked fish

Here is what some chefs like to call an all-purpose fish recipe. I don't know how all-purpose it is but I can vouch for the fact that it tastes better than many fish dishes I have had to consume.

3-4 pounds of any white fish
Butter
Juice of 2 lemons
12 small potatoes, peeled and parboiled in salted water
1/2 cup California brandy
2 tablespoons dry mustard
1 tablespoon Dijon mustard
1-1/2 cups white wine
1/4 cup capers, drained

Put the fish in a buttered casserole and sprinkle it with the lemon juice. Place the parboiled potatoes around the fish. Mix the brandy, dry mustard, Dijon mustard and white wine together and pour this sauce over the fish. Bake in a 450 degree oven for 15 to 20 minutes, or until the fish is tender. Transfer the fish and potatoes to a heated platter and keep warm. Add the capers to the sauce and cook 3 more minutes. Pour sauce over fish. Serves 6.

Chapter seven

Brandy & Vegetables

Many vegetables lend themselves to being flavored with brandy. These include carrots, mushrooms, leeks, onions, sweet potatoes, cabbage, squash, spinach, etc.

In all of these recipes, the brandy either helps the vegetable taste or increases the taste of the sauce. As with any recipe, you should adjust the amount of ingredients to suit your own tastes.

Always look for the freshest vegetables in you local store. And keep in mind the seasons, using to the best advantage those vegetables that are plentiful when in season.

Flambéed sweet potatoes

And how is brandy made?
By sheer genius, sir, sheer genius!
—ANONYMOUS

Either you like sweet potatoes or you don't. There doesn't seem to be a middle ground. However, this dish is rather different and I would suggest you try it with fried chicken.

1/3 cup butter
1/2 cup light brown sugar
1/4 cup dark corn syrup
1/2 cup orange juice
1/2 teaspoon salt
6 medium sweet potatoes, peeled, cooked and quartered
1/2 cup almonds, chopped
1/3 cup California brandy

In a large sauté pan combine the first 5 ingredients and heat to the boil. Lower heat and simmer the mixture for 5 minutes. Add potatoes and cook 10 minutes so they can become glazed. Arrange the potatoes in a medium size baking dish. Top with almonds. Heat the brandy to the sizzle, ignite and pour over the potatoes. Serves 6.

Mushrooms victor

Here is an excellent mushroom dish to serve with your favorite steak.

1 pound mushrooms, sliced
6 tablespoons butter
1/2 teaspoon salt
1 teaspoon paprika
2 tablespoons California brandy
1/2 cup heavy (whipping) cream

Melt the butter in a sauté pan or chafing dish and sauté the mushrooms until slightly brown, about 5 minutes. Add salt and paprika. Heat the brandy to the sizzle, ignite and pour over mushrooms. When flame dies out, add cream. Heat but do not boil. Serves 4-6.

Skewered mushrooms

Baked or grilled fish dishes demand a different vegetable as an accompaniment. Try these skewered mushrooms the next time a fish dish appears on your menu.

2 pounds mushrooms, stems removed
Salt and white pepper to taste
6 gratings fresh nutmeg
Olive oil
1/2 cup California brandy

Season the mushrooms with salt, pepper and the nutmeg. Thread the mushrooms equally on 6 skewers and roll them in the olive oil. Broil for 10 minutes, turning frequently. Lay the skewers in a warm shallow glass pan. Heat the brandy to the sizzle, ignite and pour over the mushrooms. Serves 6.

Carrots & walnuts

Texture is important in food presentation. Some dish may look good, but once you taste it, it leaves you wishing you had left it. Here are carrots and walnuts to please those who like a little texture in their vegetables.

8 medium carrots, cleaned, cut diagonally
1/4 cup California brandy
Water
1 tablespoon butter
Salt and white pepper to taste
1/2 cup walnuts, chopped coarsely
1/2 teaspoon dill weed

Put the carrots in a saucepan, add brandy and just enough water to barely cover the carrots. Add butter, salt and pepper. Cover and cook until the liquid is absorbed and the carrots are tender. Add walnuts and dill weed, then toss until the walnuts and dill are well mixed with the carrots. Serves 6.

Brandy sautéed mushrooms

Mushrooms are a delicate vegetable. Yet their flavor always seems to be accented with the addition of a little brandy.

1 pound mushrooms, sliced
2 tablespoons butter
1 tablespoon lemon juice
1/4 cup California brandy
1/2 teaspoon salt
1/2 teaspoon basil, crumbled
1-1/2 teaspoons cornstarch
2 tablespoons cold water
1/3 cup green onion, sliced
2 tablespoons parsley, chopped

Sauté the mushrooms in the butter with the lemon juice. Add brandy, salt and basil. Cook 2-3 minutes longer. Mix cornstarch with water and stir into the mixture. Cook until the mixture thickens, than add the onion and parsley. Cook one more minute. Stir. Serves 4.

Brandied onion slices

Onions are a great vegetable, no matter how they are cooked. I like this recipe because it can be served with game, poultry or beef.

2 tablespoons butter
2 tablespoons olive oil
4 large onions, cut in 1-inch thick slices
1 teaspoon salt
1/2 teaspoon fresh ground pepper
1/4 beef bouillon
1/4 cup California brandy

Heat the butter and oil in a saucepan. Add onions and sear for 2 minutes, turning them all the time. Add salt, pepper and bouillon and simmer for 10 minutes. Add brandy and cook another 3-4 minutes.

Broiled onion rings

If you like broiled lamb chops, this next onion dish will make them taste better.

3 large sweet onions, cut in 1/2 inch slices
3/4 cup olive oil
1/3 cup red wine vinegar
1/4 cup California brandy
1/2 teaspoon thyme
1/2 teaspoon oregano
Salt and pepper to taste

Marinate the onion slices in the remaining ingredients for 1 hour. Drain and lay the slices in a shallow pan and broil them for 5 minutes, or until they are golden brown. Put them in a serving dish and drizzle some of the marinade over the onions. Serves 4.

Leland Stanford, former governor of California and founder of the acclaimed Stanford University, had a carefully cultivated vineyard in Santa Clara County he named "Vina." According to one source the entire 1890 vintage went to his distillery for the production of brandy, making him the world's largest distiller of grape brandy in the late 1800s. He made brandy in spite of the fact that he began making wine because he considered it the best protection against the habit of drinking spirits.

Brandied carrots

1 pound large carrots, peeled and sliced thin
3 tablespoons water
4 tablespoons butter
1/2 teaspoon salt
2 tablespoons California brandy
1 teaspoon dried tarragon

In a saucepan, place the carrots, water, 3 tablespoons of the butter, salt and brandy. Cover and cook until the liquid is absorbed and the carrots are tender. Add remaining butter and top with tarragon. Mix well. Serves 6.

Carrots flambé

Here is a way to garnish that favorite roast or stew with something special. For an additional flare, do the final step in a chafing dish at the table.

12 small carrots, scraped
Water to cover
3 tablespoons sweet butter
1/4 cup California brandy

Put the carrots in a large pan with water to cover and cook them until tender, between 8-10 minutes. Drain the water. In a chafing dish melt the butter and add the carrots. Heat the brandy to the sizzle, ignite and pour over the carrots. Sauté for 2 minutes. Serves 4.

Baked carrots

If you are not in the flaming mood, here is a dish you can prepare, put in the oven for an hour and forget it.

3/4 cup butter
2 pounds carrots, scraped
Salt
1/2 teaspoon sugar
2 tablespoons California brandy

Melt the butter in a casserole, add remaining ingredients and bake 1 hour in the oven at 350 degrees. Serve the carrots with the juice from the casserole. Serves 6.

Flaming salad

Spinach salads are still in vogue. And when you flame them, they are even better. Here is a simple salad, one that I have used in my brandy demonstrations throughout the United States.

4 slices bacon, cut in 1/4-inch strips
Fresh ground black pepper to taste
3 tablespoons red wine vinegar
3 tablespoons California brandy
Enough greens (spinach, lettuce) for two

Sauté the bacon until it renders its fat and just begins to turn crisp. Add pepper, vinegar and brandy. Heat to the sizzle and ignite. Pour flaming dressing over salad. Toss well. Serves 2.

Brandied leeks

Leeks are the milder cousins in the onion family. They are the main ingredient in vichyssoise and are often served with grilled meats and fowl.

12 large leeks, washed and trimmed
4 tablespoons butter
1/4 teaspoon thyme
1/2 teaspoon salt
1/8 teaspoon black pepper
1/4 cup California brandy
1/3 cup beef bouillon
2 tablespoons lemon juice

Sauté the leeks in the butter for 2 minutes. Add remaining ingredients and cook over high heat for 10 minutes. Lower the heat to simmer and cook the leeks until they are tender. Serves 6.

Kate Warfield, one of the original and most successful women brandy-makers, was characterized by a local newspaper as "one of those energetic American ladies who is ready to take her chances with the male vineyardist, and able to hold her own." Her spirit and devotion was rewarded when her brandy won the first premium at the California State Fair in 1883. Disgruntled competitors insisted that a second test be held, which resulted in a confirmation of the original decision.

Chapter eight
Brandy &
Desserts

Brandy has always been associated with desserts. Mention brandy and people think about Crepes Suzette, Cherries Jubilee, flaming coffees, brandy and hard sauces, fruit cakes, puddings, etc.

While it is true that brandy has historically been served last, especially as an after-dinner drink and in desserts, more and more people are using brandy as an all-around cooking ingredient. These people are discovering the joy of cooking with California brandy. They are experiencing new taste treats, and they find they are liking it. They want to experiment, they want to try new ideas and they want to develop for themselves their own lifestyle.

Americans have a sweet tooth. They like desserts and there is no way that anyone is going to take them away. And so desserts laced with a little California brandy only add to pleasing and appeasing the palate.

There are so many desserts using brandy that it is hard to know where to start. So, when an author finds himself in this situation, he does everything alphabetically.

Brandy cheesecake

CAKES . . . I hadn't wanted to start this chapter with cakes because they are sort of run of the mill. But there is one cake, a cheesecake, that is excellent.

2 cups zwieback, crushed
1/8 teaspoon ground cinnamon
1/2 cup butter, plus 3 tablespoons
2-1/4 cups sugar
6 eggs, separated
3 tablespoons flour
1/4 teaspoon salt
1 teaspoon lemon juice
3 tablespoons California brandy
1 cup whole milk

Mix the zwieback, cinnamon, 1/2 cup butter and sugar together. Press the mixture into a buttered spring-formed pan. Beat the 6 yolks and add 1-3/4 cups sugar, flour and mix well. Add salt, remaining 3 tablespoons butter and lemon juice. Add brandy and gradually add the cream cheese along with the milk. Beat egg whites until they hold their peaks and fold into batter. Pour the mixture into the pie pan. Bake in a 225 degree oven for 1/2 hour. Turn off the oven and let the cake stand in the oven, door open, for 1 more hour. Chill overnight in the refrigerator. Serves 6

I like wine, both red and white and especially champagne; and on very special occasions I could even drink a small glass of brandy.
—WINSTON CHURCHILL

Chocolate truffles

A few years ago my daughter Mary Louise brought home from Bordeaux, France, some chocolate truffles. They were exquisite. I have since tasted many kinds of chocolate truffles, but few have come close to the French version. Here, from *Gourmet* magazine, is a recipe that is the closest thing to French truffles.

1 tablespoon instant expresso coffee
3 tablespoons boiling water
8 ounces semi-sweet chocolate
1/2 cup sweet butter, cut into 1/2-inch pieces
3 tablespoons California brandy
Unsweetened cocoa

One day President Lincoln heard some complaints about General Grant's drinking. Lincoln suggested that they find out what Grant was drinking so he could send a barrel to each of his generals. Grant's drink of course was brandy.

In the top of a double boiler over hot water, combine the coffee, water and chocolate. Heat the mixture until the chocolate dissolves. Take it off the heat and beat into it the butter, one piece at a time. When all the butter has been incorporated into the chocolate, add the brandy. Chill the mixture for 4 hours. Form the mixture into balls about 3/4 inch in size and roll them in the cocoa. Refrigerate them in a plastic bag. Makes 30 truffles.

Chocolate cream pots

CHOCOLATE . . . I guess this sweet is the most popular of all sweets there are in the world. Did you know that those people who adore chocolate have their own monthly publication? That's right. They get news, ideas, trends, recipes, just about anything and everything about chocolate. I must confess that I am a chocolate lover, and it gives me a great deal of pleasure to reprint this first recipe, one that appeared in my *First Brandy Cookbook*. It is rich and a little goes a long way toward topping off a fine dinner.

16-ounce package of semi-sweet chocolate chips
1 tablespoon sugar
1 egg
1 teaspoon pure vanilla extract
1 teaspoon California brandy
3/4 cup milk

Put the first five ingredients in the jar of a blender, but don't turn it on yet. Heat the milk to the boil and pour it over the contents in the blender jar. Cover and blend on high for one minute. Pour the mixture into six small custard cups and chill in the refrigerator for 4 hours. Serves 6.

Punch all livornese

COFFEE . . . Is there a restaurant in the United States that doesn't or won't serve a flaming coffee dessert? The answer is "yes" when it should be a loud "NO." Brandied coffees are known and served the world over and they are one of the great ways to end a meal. Here are some that should be in your recipe book.

In Rome's Cafe Greco on the Via Condotti, there is a warm drink named Punch all Livornese, which really isn't a punch, but that is what the owners call it. Actually, each drink is made individually.

One 4-ounce wine glass
Sugar to taste
1 small lemon peel
1/2 cup hot coffee
1 tablespoon California brandy

Preheat the glass by pouring boiling water into it. Within a few seconds the glass will be hot. Pour out the water. Add the sugar, lemon peel, coffee and brandy. Stir. Makes 1 drink.

Cafe diablo

This is my favorite coffee recipe. I like to have the lights turned off just when I am about flame it. It is really an "oh" and "ah" dish.

1 whole orange peel
15 cloves, plus 5 more
1 cup California brandy
2 cinnamon sticks, broken in half
1 thin slice lemon peel
6 cups very hot coffee

Stud the orange peel with the 15 cloves, spacing them about 3/4 inch apart. In the chafing dish, add the remaining ingredients, except the coffee. Heat the dish until the brandy sizzles. Ignite. Wrap your hand in a napkin. With a long-handled fork, hold the orange peel above the flaming mixture. With a ladle, gently let the flaming mixture run down the peel 3 or 4 times. Drop the peel into the mixture. Add the coffee which will extinguish the flame. Serves 6.

Most California brandy is aged in used oak whiskey barrels, charred on the inside. A smaller percentage is aged in new oak cooperage. The only difference is that the new oak imbues the final product with a most distinct oak flavor. The decision is the brandymaster's and depends upon his special formula.

Kona coffee

And now from the beautiful island of Hawaii, here is a special island drink.

1 ounce California brandy
1 tablespoon sugar
1 tablespoon bitter chocolate, grated
1 ounce Tia Maria liqueur
1 piece lemon peel
1 cup hot coffee
1 cinnamon stick, 6 inches long

Put the first six ingredients in a coffee cup. Add the coffee and stir with the cinnamon stick. Sip the coffee through the cinnamon stick. Makes 1 drink.

Cafe marrakech

And from the San Francisco Hilton Hotel . . .

1 ounce California brandy
1 ounce creme de cacao liqueur
6 ounces hot coffee
Fresh whipped cream
Bitter chocolate shavings

In an 8-ounce glass put the brandy and creme de cacao. Add the coffee. Spoon a large tablespoon of the whipped cream on top and dust with bitter chocolate shavings. Makes 1 drink.

Cafe royale

This is a San Francisco favorite, especially in the Italian family-style restaurants in North Beach.

2 tablespoons California brandy
1 cup hot coffee
1 cube of sugar

Float 1 tablespoon of brandy in a cup of coffee. Put the cube of sugar in a tablespoon and fill the spoon with the remaining brandy. Ignite the brandy and lower the spoon into the coffee. Stir until the flame dies. Makes 1 drink.

English brandy snaps

COOKIES . . . The most famous of all cookies using brandy are the English Brandy Snaps. Once in a while you will come across a recipe with the title Brandy Snaps only to find no brandy in the recipe. The recipe below has brandy in it and is believed to have come over from England on the Mayflower.

1-1/2 cups flour, sifted
1/4 teaspoon salt
2 teaspoons powdered ginger
1/4 teaspoon fresh grated nutmeg
3/4 cup butter
1 cup brown sugar
1/2 cup molasses
1/4 cup California brandy

Mix the flour, salt, ginger and nutmeg and resift. Mix the butter, sugar, molasses and brandy. Mix with flour. Drop teaspoonsful of the batter onto a buttered cookie sheet. Leave about 2 inches between cookies. Bake 12 minutes in a 300 degree oven. Makes 48 cookies.

Black walnut brandy cookies

Black walnuts lend a distinctive flavor to anything they come in contact with. And when introduced to California brandy, they make a memorable dessert.

1 cup butter
1 cup confectioners sugar, plus 3 tablespoons
3 tablespoons California brandy
1 teaspoon pure vanilla extract
2 cups flour
1/4 teaspoon salt
1 cup black walnuts, chopped fine

Cream the butter with the cup of sugar using an electric mixer. Add brandy and vanilla and mix well. Add remaining ingredients. Shape mixture into 1-inch balls. Place the balls about 2 inches apart on an ungreased cookie sheet. Bake 20 minutes at 325 degrees. Dust the cookies with the remaining sugar. Makes 48 cookies.

Crepes suzette

CREPES . . . The most dramatic as well as one of the most famous of all the desserts in the world is Crepes Suzette. Its creator, Henri Charpentier, was only 15 years old when he created the famous dessert. He was working at the Café de Paris in Monte Carlo, as an assistant waiter. One of his duties was to help Edward, Prince of Wales, choose a menu.

One evening, he bragged to the prince, who was known for his exceptional palate, that the prince would taste a sweet never before served to anyone. Now that was quite a boast for a lad of 15, but it was done with true French arrogance. Henri was about to make a name for himself, one that the world would not forget.

Everything Henri was doing was perfect. The crepes never looked better. Suddenly, some of the liqueurs he was using caught on fire. He never flinched. He tasted the sauce and knew he had won. Boldly, he added more liqueurs and flamed them. When the flames died, he served the Prince his new creation.

The Prince asked him what he called the new creation and young Henri replied, "Crepes Princess." The prince asked him to change the name to Suzette, in honor of the young lady the prince was dining with. Henri agreed and that is how the dish was created and named, all in one night before the future King of England.

4 cubes of sugar
1 orange
1/2 cup butter
3 tablespoons California brandy
3 tablespoons curacao
3 tablespoons kirsch
12 dessert crepes

Squeeze the orange and reserve the juice and peel. With a sharp knife, make several cuts on the surface of the orange peel and rub the cubes of sugar on the orange peel until the sugar has absorbed the oil of the orange. Crush the sugar cubes and mix with half the butter until creamy. In a chafing dish, melt the remaining butter and mix with sugar/butter mixture. Add orange juice, brandy, curacao, kirsch and heat until it sizzles. Ignite. When the flame dies, add the crepes 2 at a time. Serve the crepes well covered with the sauce. May be served with ice cream or whipped cream (optional). Serves 6.

Lemon crepes

Lemon and crepes make an interesting combination. This next recipe is from Portugal.

8 dessert crepes
3/4 cup sugar
2 teaspoons grated lemon rind
2 tablespoons butter, plus 1/2 cup
1/4 cup California brandy
1/4 cup orange-flavored liqueur
2 tablespoons lemon juice

Fold the crepes in half and lay them on a buttered and flameproof dish. Sprinkle the crepes with the sugar and lemon rind. Dot them with 2 tablespoons of butter. Broil the crepes until the sugar has melted and is bubbling. In a saucepan melt the remaining butter and add the brandy, orange-flavored liqueur and lemon juice. Heat the sauce and mix well. Serve the sauce over the crepes. Serves 6.

Crepes flambés

Here is a quick and easy crepe recipe, one that you can complete in less than 15 minutes.

12 dessert crepes
1/2 cup prune-flavored liqueur
4 tablespoons sugar
4 tablespoons butter
4 tablespoons water
1 teaspoon grated orange peel
1/4 cup California brandy

Fold the crepes in four and arrange them in a buttered chafing dish. In a separate pan, heat together the remaining ingredients, except the brandy. Pour the heated sauce over the crepes and heat for 2 minutes. Heat the brandy to the sizzle, ignite and pour the flaming spirit over the crepes. When the flame dies, spoon some of the sauce over the crepes. Serves 6.

Brandied fruitcake

Famed artist, W.G. Tiffany, who spent many years in France, declared General Naglee's California brandy as "superior to any brandy I have ever tasted" and ordered five gallons.

FRUITCAKE . . . A holiday favorite, fruitcake has long been associated with brandy. Here is one of the best fruitcake recipes I have ever worked with or tasted. It makes two large cakes or four small ones if you like and with the addition of a little brandy every two weeks, they should keep until next Christmas. Again, a tip of the chef's hat to *Gourmet* magazine, where this recipe first appeared many years ago.

2 cups butter
2 cups brown sugar
9 whole eggs
6-1/2 cups flour, sifted
1-1/2 tablespoons baking powder
1 tablespoon of equal parts of cinnamon, allspice, cloves and fresh grated nutmeg
2 cups California brandy
2 pounds currants
1/2 pound candied cherries
1/2 pound almonds, blanched
1/4 pound mixed orange and lemon peel

Cream the butter, add the brown sugar and mix until light and fluffy. Add the eggs, well beaten. Add the 6 cups of flour, baking powder and mixed spices along with the brandy. In the remaining flour, lightly toss the currants, cherries, almonds and orange/lemon peel until they are well coated. Add them to the mixture. When the mixture is blended, line two large loaf pans with buttered heavy brown paper. Pour in the batter and bake 2 hours at 250 degrees, or until they test done.

Flaming grapes

GRAPES . . . Brandy is distilled from pure California grape juice. It is fitting that I include at least one flaming dish using grapes.

Juice of 1 orange
Rind of 1 orange
1/4 cup sugar
3 cups seedless grapes
1/2 cup California brandy

In a chafing dish cook the juice, rind and sugar for 5 minutes to make a syrup. Add the grapes and cook for 1 minute, stirring constantly. Heat the brandy to the sizzle, ignite and pour over grapes. Serve with vanilla ice cream. Serves 6.

Paradise

ICE CREAM . . . "I scream, you scream, we all scream for ice cream." Forty years ago, kids all over America were singing this little ditty. It nearly became the national anthem for desserts. Today ice cream is probably the number one dessert for most people.

Here are a few tips in dealing with ice cream.
- Always leave ice cream in the carton when storing it in the refrigerator.
- Never slice factory-packed ice cream; always spoon it out. This way you will knock out some of the air in the ice cream and it will taste better.
- Manufacturers agree that the best storage temperature for ice cream is between 6 and 10 degrees above zero.

This first recipe is a delightful way to end a meal. After they taste this dessert, they will want more and you may just have to skip coffee.

1 quart of the best French vanilla ice cream
1/3 bottle of California brandy

Put both ingredients in a blender and whip together until smooth. Pour into small brandy snifters. Serves 6.

Civil War Veteran, Henry Morris Naglee, visited France and studied brandy making in great depth. He returned to San Jose, California in 1876, planted top quality grape varieties, built a distillery and embarked on the goal of producing California's finest Brandy. He won a number of awards and medals and his famed Naglia brandy was declared the finest at the Centennial Exposition in 1878.

Brandy ice cream

Here is an ice cream dessert that can even take a little extra spirit in the final presentation.

10 egg yolks
1-1/2 cups sugar
4 cups milk
4 cups heavy (whipping) cream
3/4 cup California brandy

Whisk the eggs and sugar in a saucepan until they are thick and lemon in color. In a separate pan, bring the milk and cream to just below the boil. Gradually add the milk/cream mixture to the yolk mixture, beating constantly. Cook the sauce until it resembles a thin custard. Continue stirring after the sauce has been removed from the heat. Cool and chill. Pour the sauce into the container of an electric or hand-cranked ice cream freezer. Add brandy. Freeze according to manufacturer's instructions. Serves 12.

Brandy peaches

PEACHES . . . One of the great fruits of America, nothing tastes better than a fresh ripe peach just picked off the tree. However, chefs, in their never-ending search for better and better ideas, have mated fresh peaches and California brandy.

6 ripe peaches
1/4 cup sugar
1/3 cup California brandy

Peel the peaches, halve them and discard the stones. Place the peaches in a flameproof dish. Sprinkle them with the sugar. Heat the brandy to the sizzle, ignite and pour the flaming spirit over the peaches. Serve immediately. Serves 6.

Peaches st. hubert

And if you don't want to flame peaches . . .

1/2 cup California brandy
1/4 cup dark corn syrup
1/2 teaspoon pure almond extract
6 ripe peaches
2 tablespoons honey
Fresh grated nutmeg to taste

Put the first three ingredients in a saucepan and boil to make a syrup for just 1 minute. Peel and halve the peaches. Poach the peaches in the syrup for 5 minutes. Drain the peaches and arrange them on a serving platter. Reduce the syrup until it becomes thick. Add the honey and nutmeg. Pour sauce over the peaches. Serves 6.

Flaming pineapple rings

PINEAPPLE . . . Ever hear of a flaming pineapple dessert? Well, they serve it in the West Indies and the recipe goes like this—

1 ripe pineapple, peeled, cored and cut in 1/2-inch slices
1/4 cup flour
1/2 cup milk
3 tablespoons clarified butter
Cherries
1/4 cup sugar
1/4 cup California brandy

Dredge the rings first in flour, then milk and back in the flour again. Sauté the rings in the butter until they become golden brown on both sides. Remove to a flameproof platter and insert a cherry in the center of each ring. Sprinkle with sugar and bake in a 400 degree oven until the sugar bubbles and begins to carmelize. Heat the brandy to the sizzle, ignite and pour the flaming spirit over the rings. Serve the pineapple while it is still flaming. Serves 6.

A cowboy saunters into the saloon, bellies up to the bar and barks, "Gimme a shot of Red-Eye!" A bartender in a Hollywood movie would serve this cowpoke whiskey, but the drink most often requested in a real bar during the 1800s was brandy that probably came from California.

Perigord pudding

PUDDING . . . There are all kinds of puddings: custard, rice, beef, plum, bread, cake—seems just about anything can be turned into a pudding. In the south of France, in the Perigord region, there is a pudding speciality served in almost all the homes. It is a dish made up of baked crepe batter filled with brandy-soaked prunes and raisins and served very hot.

2 ounces raisins
1/2 pound prunes, pitted
1/4 cup California brandy
1/2 cup sugar
4 eggs
Pinch of salt
1/2 cup flour
1 cup milk
1/2 teaspoon pure vanilla extract
2 tablespoons butter

Plump the raisins in hot water for 10 minutes. Drain. Cut the prunes in half. Combine the prunes and raisins in a glass jar and add the brandy. Cover tightly. Turn the jar over every hour for 8 hours. Beat the sugar, eggs, and salt together in a bowl. Sift the flour and slowly whisk it into the mixture. Add milk, extract and contents from the jar. Liberally butter a Pyrex pie plate and pour the batter into it. Bake 20 minutes in a 400 degree oven. Serve hot. Serves 6.

Citron pudding

This is an English pudding, not often served in the United States. If you like to surprise your guests or have guests that are English, try this treat.

6 egg yolks
2 tablespoons flour
2 cups whole milk
1/2 cup California brandy
4 ounces citron
2 tablespoons sugar

Beat the yolks until they are light and stir in the flour. Gradually add the milk, brandy, citron and sugar. Mix the batter until smooth. Butter 6 custard cups and pour the batter in them. Bake 20 minutes at 400 degrees. Serves 6.

Brandy sauce

Here is an all-purpose brandy sauce for just about any pudding you can make. I have yet to find a pudding that this sauce didn't help.

1 stick of butter, room temperature
2 cups confectioners sugar
1/4 cup California brandy

Cream the butter with the confectioners sugar. When well mixed, gradually add the brandy until you have a smooth sauce. Makes 1 cup.

Bread pudding

Now that we have the sauce, how about the bread pudding.

2 cups milk
1/2 stick butter
1/2 cup sugar
4 cups of day-old bread, (French/Italian is best)
1/2 cup raisins
2 eggs, beaten
1/2 teaspoon fresh grated nutmeg
1 teaspoon pure vanilla extract

Scald the milk. Melt the butter in the hot milk. Stir in the sugar. Pour over bread and raisins and let stand for 15 minutes. Add remaining ingredients and mix well. Pour the batter into a buttered 1-1/2-quart dish and bake 35 minutes at 350 degrees. Serve with the Brandy Sauce. Serves 6.

Before the advent of aspirin and anesthetics, brandy and rum were used to ease the aches and pains of illness. And, if alcohol "cured" a disease or so went the logic then it would work equally as well as a preventative. Thus, many a colonial planter would begin his day with a glass or two of punch made with brandy.

Brandy sauce 1

SAUCES . . . There are many sweet brandy sauces, all a little different, but all important for any chef's notebook. They go with hundreds of dishes.

4 tablespoons butter
1 cup confectioners sugar
1/4 cup California brandy
2 egg yolks, well beaten
1/2 cup heavy (whipping) cream
Whites of two eggs, beaten stiff

In a pan, cream the butter and gradually add the sugar. When blended, add brandy, yolks and cream. Cook the mixture in the top of a double boiler over hot water constantly stirring until it thickens. Pour the mixture over the whites and whisk until well blended. Makes about 1 cup.

Brandy sauce 2

2 eggs separated
1 cup sugar
1/4 cup California brandy

In a bowl beat the yolks with half the sugar until they are lemon-colored. Slowly beat in the brandy. In another bowl, beat the whites with the remaining sugar until they hold their peaks. Fold the white mixture into the egg mixture. Serve with steamed puddings.

Brandy sauce 3

1 cup light brown sugar
1/2 cup heavy (whipping) cream
1/4 cup butter
1/2 teaspoon salt
6 tablespoons California brandy

In a saucepan, cook the first four ingredients for 3 minutes. Remove the sauce from the heat and add the brandy. Mix well. Serve this hot sauce with puddings or souffles. Makes 1-1/2 cups.

Mocha brandy sauce

6 ounces sweet chocolate
1/2 ounce bitter chocolate
1/2 cup strong coffee
1 tablespoon California brandy

Melt the two chocolates in the coffee, stirring constantly. Add brandy and mix well. Serve hot with ice cream. Makes about 1-1/2 cups.

Chocolate brandy sauce

12-ounce package semi-sweet chocolate
2 squares unsweetened chocolate
3 tablespoons coffee
1/2 pint heavy (whipping) cream
3 tablespoons California brandy

In a double boiler melt the two chocolates with the coffee. Gradually stir in the cream and brandy. Stir until mixture is smooth. Makes 2 cups.

One of the more inventive men in the history of the brandy industry was George Malter. He not only produced an excellent tasting brandy at his Fresno vineyards but during the 1890s also attempted to create a new market for the spirit by selling "Bathing Brandy" that was guaranteed to stimulate the nerves, strengthen the muscles, and nourish and improve the skin.

Bathing Brandy

Grape brandy, rich in essential oils, for the use of the bath, is a medical innovation and modern luxury.

Every bath should certainly contain a supply of this grape brandy.

Brandy used on the skin after the taking of a cold or hot water bath, has a strangely pleasant and greatly beneficial effect on the body and mind.

Grape brandy containing a large percentage of fine essential oils of the grape, will be found of much more medical value in the external application to the the skin than ordinary alcohol. Alcohol stimulates the nerves, essential oils serve to strengthen the muscles. These oils not only nourish and improve the skin but they impart direct nourishment to the flesh through the skin. It will be found that parts of the body treated with grape brandy rich in grape oils, will be perceptibly developed and strengthened.

Massage treatment with this brandy will physically improve the condition of the skin, render it soft, glossy, clear and almost translucent, hence the use of grape brandy for sponge bath purposes, is not only one of the greatest luxuries of the age, but it is also one of the most beneficial of the

uses of stimulants, serving as it does to sustain and restore the strength of body and mind. Alcoholic stimulants cannot in all cases be taken to advantage through the stomach, whilst some diseases, ailments and weaknesses call for internal use of alcoholic stimulants; other disorders are sometimes aggravated thereby; moreover the abuse of strong drink is to be feared, since the nerves are easily over-stimulated. On the other hand, the external use of alcohol, or better, grape brandy, is not subject to these objections.

The ancient Romans knew of no luxuries as great as that of the use of grape brandy for the bath. No bath can be more beneficial than the brandy bath. The expense of using brandy at the bath is not by any means great since a quart costing a dollar will last a month, reasonably used by one person. Our bathing brandy is almost twice as strong in grape spirits than the brandy for internal use and it con-

ins about 10 per cent of the essential oils of the grape.
Price per case of 12 qts...............$10 00

Sauce lorette

Here are two different sauces that have a unique taste. You can try them on a variety of dishes.

4 egg yolks
1/2 cup sugar
1/4 cup California brandy
1/3 teaspoon orange flower water
1/2 cup cream, whipped

Beat the yolks and sugar together until they become thick and pale in color. Cook over hot water for 5 minutes, stirring constantly. Take the custard off the heat and beat in the brandy and orange flower water. Chill and then fold in the whipped cream.

Red wine sauce

1-1/2 cups red wine
1/2 cup California brandy
3 tablespoons lemon juice
1 tablespoon cornstarch
2 tablespoons cold water
Pinch ground cinnamon
Pinch ground cloves
Sugar to taste

In a saucepan combine the wine, brandy and lemon juice. Mix the cornstarch and water and add it to the sauce pan. Add cinnamon and cloves. Bring the sauce to the boil. Remove from the heat and add sugar to taste. Makes 2 cups.

Brown sugar hard sauce

2/3 cup butter, softened
2 cups brown sugar
2 egg yolks
3 tablespoons California brandy

In a bowl cream together the butter and sugar. Stir in the yolks and add the brandy. Beat the mixture until it is light and fluffy. Excellent with puddings. Makes 3 cups.

California's San Joaquin Valley, where most of the grapes used for brandy making are grown was once a barren, uninhabitable wasteland. The famous scout, Kit Carson, led expeditions through this valley that also served as a hiding place for such notorious criminals as Black Bart and Joaquin Murieta. Beginning in the early 1800s, determined groups of immigrants tamed the wilderness and made it the richest agricultural area of its size in the world.

Chapter nine
Brandy
Punches & Eggnog

You say you get nervous at the thought of concocting a punch? Then consider the dilemma Sir Edward Kennel, commander-in-chief of the English Royal Navy, faced when making a punch for 6,000 guests in 1599.

In a huge marble basin, he mixed 80 casks of brandy, nine casks of water, 25,000 large limes, 80 pints of lemon juice, 1,300 pounds of sugar, five pounds of ground nutmeg and 300 biscuits. He topped off the punch with a giant cask of Malaga wine.

The punch was served by the ship's boys who literally sailed on a sea of punch in small rosewood boats. The fumes from the alcohol were so powerful that Sir Edward had to replace the boys every 15 minutes, lest they keel over and fall into the mixture.

The word punch is believed to come from the Hindustani "panch" which means "five," indicating the number of actual ingredients used: Arrack (a type of brandy), tea, sugar, water and lemon juice. The punch bowl itself is probably of Oriental origin and was borrowed by the Americans from the English.

Early Americans loved punch. George Washington, Alexander Hamilton, Benjamin Franklin and others often proffered good feelings by serving a punch made of rum, brandy, curacao, lemon, hot water, grated nutmeg, cloves and cinnamon. Indeed, a Mr. William Black wrote in his diary on a visit to Philadelphia in 1774: "I was given cider and punch for lunch, rum and brandy before dinner, punch, Madeira, port and sherry at dinner, bounce and liqueurs with the ladies, and wine, spirits and punch until bedtime."

Proper Boston folks, according to one writer of that period ". . . served a great punch bowl before dinner. If the bowl were not too large it was passed from hand to hand, and all drank from it without the ceremony of intervening glasses."

Punches can be kept cold in two ways—by pre-chilling all the ingredients and by using a block of ice. Always use block ice because ice cubes dilute the punch too fast. If you can't buy blocks of ice, you can make them yourself. Wash out a half gallon milk carton. Fill it with water, add a few pieces of fruit and lay it on its side in the freezer for three hours.

It is not necessary to use conventional punch bowls. Be daring. Have you ever seen one of those giant brandy snifters that look like they could seat three people? They make excellent punch bowls.

The success of any punch is only as good as the ingredients you use. Always use the best. And when serving punch, figure at least three 4-ounce cups per person.

For a complete collection of brandy drink recipes; over 500 cocktails, coolers, punches, hot drinks, dessert drinks and holiday nogs see: CALIFORNIA BRAND DRINKS book by Malcolm R. Hébert. Published 1981 by The Wine Appreciation Guild, $4.95.

Champagne punch a l'antoine's

Antoine's in New Orleans is a gastronomic landmark in a city that knows good food. On special occasions, Antoine's will serve their creation, a very good punch which they ladle out in generous portions.

1 fifth champagne
1 fifth sauterne
1/4 pound confectioners sugar
1 pint sparkling water
1 cup California brandy
2 ounces maraschino liqueur
2 ounces Cointreau
Block of ice
Thin slices of orange peel and pineapple

Mix well in a punch bowl. Add ice and orange peels and pineapple. Makes 25-30 servings.

It was "guaranteed to make a dancer out of someone who had never even set foot on a dance floor," according to President Andrew Jackson. He was referring to a mixture of brandy, champagne, rum, tea, lemon, sugar and arrack. He named it Daniel Webster Punch, and rumor has that it indeed packed quite a wallop.

Fish house punch

Fish House Punch was said to have been originated in 1732 at the Old Philadelphia Club. It makes a great Sunday punch.

3/4 pound sugar
3-1/2 pints water
1-1/2 pints lemon juice
2 fifths rum
1 fifth California brandy
3 ounces peach brandy
Block of ice

Mix the sugar and water until the sugar is dissolved. Add remaining ingredients and let marry for several hours. Put a large block of ice in a punch bowl and add the mixture. Serves 12.

Artillery punch

I suspect just about everybody has his or her favorite artillery punch recipe. But do you know that it was named artillery punch because it was a favorite punch of the men in the artillery and not because of the kick it can give you?

1 fifth rye whiskey
1 bottle red wine
6 cups black tea
1 pint rum
1/2 pint gin
1/2 pint California brandy
1 pint orange juice
1/2 pint lemon juice
4 ounces Benedictine
Block of ice

Mix well and allow to ripen for several hours. Put a block of ice in a punch bowl and pour mixture over it. Serves 24.

Midnight punch

It always seems to me that anything served at midnight ought to be special—like this next punch.

1 fifth California brandy
1/2 cup lemon juice
1/3 cup sugar syrup
3 fifths champagne
20 whole strawberries
Block ice

Combine the first three ingredients and pour them over the block of ice in a punch bowl. Slowly add the champagne and float the strawberries in the mixture. Makes 25 servings.

Brandy milk punch

Milk punches, thanks to the creamy liqueurs that have come on the market, are making a comeback. Here is an excellent afternoon libation.

8 ounces California brandy
4 cups whole milk
2 tablespoons sugar
1 tray ice cubes
Nutmeg, fresh ground

Have the brandy and the milk well chilled. Combine both with the sugar and ice cubes. Stir together until the mixture is very cold. Discard ice cubes. Pour into chilled glasses and dust with nutmeg. Serve 4-6.

Cassis punch

Many years ago the then-mayor of Chablis, devised a drink made with Cassis and Chablis wine. He called it a Kir and it became very popular. You can do the same thing except you use champagne and California brandy.

4 cups club soda
2 cups Cassis
1 cup California brandy
2 fifths champagne
Block ice

Combine the first three ingredients and pour over the block ice in a punch bowl. Add the champagne. Makes 30 servings.

The Grand Experiment, Prohibition, made into law by Congress in 1919 nearly destroyed the brandy industry—but not quite. The federal government did issue a few permits for limited brandy production for "medicinal" purposes. It was possible during Prohibition for a person to obtain a physician's prescription to purchase spirits—whiskey or brandy—and many such prescriptions were issued.

Merry mens punch

If you are going to have a large number of people over for punch and cookies, here is a punch that will handle 25 people with no trouble at all.

1 quart pineapple juice
1 cup lime juice
1 cup sugar
1 tablespoon orange bitters
1 fifth white wine
1 fifth California brandy
3 fifths champagne
20 small fresh pineapple sticks
Block ice

In a mixing bowl combine the first four ingredients and stir until the sugar is dissolved. Add wine and brandy. Chill. Pour mixture over block ice in a punch bowl and add champagne. Garnish with pineapple sticks. Makes 50 four-ounce servings. NOTE: If you cannot get orange bitters, Angostura bitters will suffice.

Glogg

No punch section in any cookbook would be complete without a recipe for glogg, the Swedish national libation. Here is one that will neatly fill your cup.

2 teaspoons sugar
2 whole cloves
1 piece cinnamon stick, 2 inches long
6 raisins
1-1/2 ounces California brandy
1 teaspoon dry sherry

Put all the ingredients in a stainless steel pan. Heat the mixture until the brandy sizzles. Ignite and when the flame dies, add the Sherry. Serve in metal cup. Makes 1 drink.

Holiday milk punch

I like to think of this punch as one that can be served year-round. Of course, any punch can be served throughout the year; but this one, a milk punch, seems right for the holidays.

2-1/2 quarts milk
1 quart California brandy
1 pint creme de cacao
Fresh grated nutmeg

Combine the first three ingredients in a large bowl set over shaved ice to keep the mixture cold. Serve the punch in cold punch cups. Dust each serving with the nutmeg. Makes 30 four-ounce servings.

Champagne punch

This has to be the fastest punch in the world. Moreover, it tastes like it took hours to assemble.

1 fifth champagne, chilled
1/2 cup California brandy
1/2 cup orange-flavored liqueur
1/2 bottle sparkling water, chilled

Combine all the ingredients in a large bowl and serve the mixture in small chilled punch cups. Makes 15 servings.

Even great generals got involved with brandy. One such general was Mariano Guadalupe Vallejo. He was a fierce rival of Agoston Haraszthy and boldly marketed his brandy throughout California. It was reputed to be of excellent quality and taste.

Tom & jerry

The most famous of all eggnogs is Tom and Jerry. I first tasted a Tom and Jerry one Christmas week when I was a reporter for the *Chicago Daily News,* many years ago. Some public relations people were having their annual party for all press people and I got an invitation to attend. The Empire Room of the Palmer House was decorated in Christmas colors and there were at least three huge silver bowls filled to the top with foamy Tom and Jerries.

I tasted one and thought that it wasn't very strong, a nice holiday drink, easy to take. The next day I thought I would make some for friends and after a recipe search found there is no one recipe for a Tom and Jerry, but hundreds. Well, over the years I have collected quite a few T&J recipes, but I think this one is the best.

6 eggs, separated
1 cup sugar
1-1/2 teaspoons allspice
1-1/2 teaspoons cinnamon
1-1/2 teaspoons cloves
1/4 cup dark rum
1/4 cup California brandy (per drink), warmed, plus 1 teaspoon
Hot milk

In a bowl beat the yolks, sugar and spices until light. Add rum, beating again. In a separate bowl beat the whites until they are stiff and fold in egg mixture. For each drink, put 1/2 cup of the egg mixture and 1/4 cup California brandy in a warm Tom & Jerry mug. Fill the mug with hot milk. Stir until well mixed. Float 1 teaspoon of California brandy on top. Makes enough egg mixture for 15 drinks.

In the 1830s, father Narciso Durán at Mission San José became an accomplished brandy maker. Hubert H. Bancroft described his brandy as "double distilled and as strong as the reverend father's faith".

Eggnog one

Here are two brandy eggnog recipes that make a single drink. Both recipes can be doubled, tripled or more without changing the measurements.

1 teaspoon sugar
1 egg yolk
1-1/2 ounces California brandy
1/2 cup milk
Ice
Fresh grated nutmeg

Put everything except the nutmeg into a cocktail shaker and shake well. Strain into a 10-ounce glass. Dust with nutmeg. Makes 1 drink.

Aging wine and brandy, a common practice in France, was a revolutionary development when it was introduced to California vintners by Louis Vignes in the 1830s. Formerly, these beverages were made carelessly and stored in unclean containers so that they became unfit for drinking before they had a chance to age.

Eggnog two

1-1/2 ounces California brandy
1 ounce dark rum
2 teaspoons bar syrup
1/2 cup cold milk
1 egg
Cinnamon

Put the ingredients in a cocktail shaker and fill with cracked ice. Shake until well mixed. Strain into a highball glass. Dust with cinnamon. Makes 1 drink.

A warm nog

And if you like a hot eggnog . . .

1 egg yolk
1 teaspoon sugar
1 ounce California brandy
1 ounce rum
Milk
Fresh grated nutmeg

In a heated mug, combine the first four ingredients. Heat the milk and pour it into the mug to fill it. Stir constantly. Top with nutmeg. Makes 1 drink.

Frozen brandy eggnog

For a different treat, how about a frozen brandy eggnog.

12 egg yolks
2-1/2 cups sugar
3 quarts heavy (whipping) cream, whipped
1-1/2 cups California brandy
1 cup dark rum

Beat the yolks until they are thick and gradually beat in the sugar. Fold in the whipped cream. Freeze the mixture until almost hard. Remove and let it soften. Mix in brandy and rum and refreeze. Serve the frozen eggnog in small punch cups with spoons. Serves 12.

Wfb eggnog

Now here is the world's fastest brandy eggnog.

1 teaspoon sugar
1 egg yolk
1-1/2 ounces California brandy
1/2 cup milk

Combine mixture in a small bowl. Whisk until frothy. Pour into a highball glass. Makes 1 drink.

Chapter ten

Brandy &
Potpourri

What follows is a medley of things, recipes that use California brandy but don't seem to fit into any one category.

I have not put them in any particular order. They are included in this book because they are good recipes and once again show the versatility of California brandy in everyday cooking.

Brandy cream pie

Americans love pies. It doesn't make much difference what kind of pie it is, just as long as it is pie. This love goes back to our founding fathers, who brought with them their pie-making abilities. I have often thought about what the American Indian must have felt the first time he bit into a pumpkin pie. What a story that would have made.

1 cup chocolate wafers, crushed
1/4 cup brown sugar
1/3 cup butter, melted
6 egg yolks
1 cup sugar
1 tablespoon gelatin
1/2 cup cold water
2 cups heavy (whipping) cream
1/2 cup California brandy
Shaved bitter chocolate

Agoston Haraszthy, the legendary figure of early California viticulture, settled in Sonoma and built a still in front of his cellars. When he imported thousands of vine cuttings from Europe in the 1860s, he explained that "it was the foreign grapes which were going to produce not only finer wines, but better brandies."

Mix the crushed wafers, brown sugar and butter thoroughly. Line a deep pie plate with the crumbs and chill 20 minutes in the refrigerator. Beat the yolks with the sugar until the mixture is thick. Soak the gelatin in the water, stir over hot water until the gelatin is completely mixed. Gradually add to the gelatin the egg mixture. Whip the cream until stiff and then fold into the egg mixture, then add the brandy, stirring. Place the mixture over cracked ice and stir until it begins to set. Pour it into the pie shell and chill until firm. Top with shavings. Serves 6.

Brandy pralines

One of the most delightful edibles ever to grace the tables of the South are pralines. The little sugared pecan tidbits are welcome anytime and in our house gobbled up before they can cool. You can purchase them throughout the South and they are good. But I think these pralines are the best you will ever sink your teeth into.

The department of Viticulture and Enology at the University of California at Davis is the only school in the United States to teach students the art of brandymaking. The course, "Brandy 140," has an enrollment of two dozen or more each year.

1 cup white sugar
1 cup brown sugar
1/3 cup California brandy
1/3 cup half and half
1 cup pecan halves
1 tablespoon butter

In a heavy saucepan, melt the sugars in the brandy and half and half. Cook the mixture over medium heat until a candy thermometer registers 236 degrees. Remove the pan from the heat and stir in the pecans and the butter. Let the mixture cool for 2 or 3 minutes and beat it until it starts to thicken. Quickly drop the mixture by tablespoons onto a buttered wax paper or foil. Let the waferlike pralines cool and harden before removing them from the paper. Makes about 15 pralines.

Brandy & bows

One does not ordinarily associate brandy with spaghetti. Yet there are dishes that do have brandy in them, especially in this sauce. Because this recipe uses the Italian "farfalle" which are pieces of pasta shaped like little bow ties, I have called this dish Brandy and Bows.

16-ounce package of farfalle
1 tablespoon olive oil
6 tablespoons butter
1/2 cup California brandy
Salt and white pepper to taste
1 clove garlic, cut in half
1-1/2 cups fresh grated Parmesan cheese

Cook the little bows in hot water for 8 minutes. In a small bowl, cream the butter, brandy, salt and pepper. With the clove of garlic rub the inside of a bowl to gently coat it with a touch of garlic. When the bows are cooked, drain them. Put them in the garlic-scented bowl and top with cheese. Add butter/brandy mixture and toss until all is well mixed. Serves 4.

Brandy mayonnaise

Have you been looking for a sauce to go with cold meats? Well, try this one.

1 egg
1 hard boiled egg, riced
6 tablespoons olive oil
1 teaspoon dry mustard
1 teaspoon sugar
1 tablespoon California brandy
Salt and white paper to taste

Beat the eggs with the oil drop by drop and mix well. Add the mustard and sugar and whisk again. Add the brandy, salt and pepper, whisking again. Makes 1/2 cup.

Alfredo's sauce

After prohibition, the Jesuits resumed brandy making at their Novitiate winery at Villa Maria. Their small 190 gallon capacity still produced brandy primarily for fortifying sacramental wines but some always found its way to "medicinal use".

"I am a pasta freak," said the lady sitting next to me at a recent dinner party. "My husband and I lived in Rome for a year and I got hooked on the stuff. My problem is that I want sauces other than just those made with tomatoes."

I suppose it is true that there are more tomato-based sauces for pasta than any other kind. I thought about her problem and remembered a sauce I had been served in Milan many years ago.

It had been a hard day in Milan. I had interviewed almost a dozen manufacturers for a magazine story I was assigned to do. My Italian was terrible so I had to rely on translators. The back and forth exchanges had tired me out.

I showered, changed clothes and went down to the hotel dining room. After a Campari and soda, I told my waiter Alfredo that I wanted just a small supper, maybe a simple spaghetti with a sauce and a bottle of Frascati, fruit and cheese for dessert and that was it. He nodded and left.

Now Alfredo is not the typical Italian waiter. He was quiet. He listened to what you wanted. He made suggestions only if you asked for his opinion. And if you knew what you wanted he was perfectly willing to serve you what you ordered.

Alfredo opened the bottle of Frascati. He served the hot buttered spaghetti and poured over it a pale yellow, basil-flavored sauce which he quickly tossed to coat the thin strains of pasta. He waited until I tasted the first bite. It was ambrosia. I asked him what it was and he said it was just a Hollandaise with pesto.

That was a dozen years ago. Since then I have been working on such a recipe and have devised one that is almost as good as the one Alfredo served me. Because Alfredo was generous enough to explain the sauce in a little more detail, I have named my version after him.

4 egg yolks
2 teaspoons lemon juice
2 cloves garlic, minced
1/2 teaspoon dried basil, crushed
1/4 cup parsley, minced
3/4 cup sweet butter
4 tablespoons California brandy
1/2 cup fresh grated Pecorino or Parmesan cheese

Combine yolks, lemon juice, garlic, basil and parsley in a blender jar and blend 5 seconds. Heat the butter until very hot. Put blender on high speed and dribble the hot butter into the egg mixture. When well mixed pour into a bowl. Add the brandy and cheese and whisk until well blended. Makes 1-1/2 cups.

PHOTO CREDITS

We gratefully acknowledge the use of photos from:

Bancroft Library, University of California, Berkeley, CA.

The Wine Museum of San Francisco, CA "The Christian Brothers Collection".

Wine Institute, San Francisco, CA.

CALIFORNIA WINERIES, NAPA VALLEY, published by Vintage Image.

CALFORNIA WINERIES, SONOMA & MENDOCINO, published by Vintage Image.

IN CELEBRATION OF WINE & LIFE, published by The Wine Appreciation Guild.

INDEX

#641 THE POCKET ENCYCLOPEDIA OF CALIFORNIA WINE by William I. Kaufman. A convenient and thorough reference book that fits into your vest pocket and gives answers to all of your questions about California Wines. All the wineries, grape varieties, wines, geography and wine terms are covered briefly and authoritatively by one of America's foremost wine experts. Carry with you to restaurants and wine tastings to make you well informed on your choice of California Wines. 236 compact pages, 7¾″ x 3½″ with vinyl cover. $4.95 @ ISBN 0-932664-09-1, 1983 Latest Edition.

#671 CORKSCREWS, KEYS TO HIDDEN PLEASURES by Manfred Heckman and A.K. Rodenaker. The first authoritative book on corkscrews, their history, science, design and enjoyment: for the connoisseur or the novice. Over 500 corkscrew models are covered with a multitude of photos and 10 full color pages. Essential for the collector and fascinating for anyone interested in wine. 124 pp, color cover. English edition available 1984, $20.00 @ ISBN 0-032664-17-2.

#672 THE CALIFORNIA WINE DRINK BOOK by William I. Kaufman. Cocktails, hot drinks, punches and coolers all made with wine. Over 200 different drink recipes, using various wines along with mixing tips and wine entertaining suggestions. Today's accent on lighter drinks makes this a most useful handbook, and you'll save money too by using wine rather than higher taxed liquors! Pocket size, leatherette cover, 128 pp, $4.95. May 1982, ISBN 0-932664-10-9.

#673 WINE IN EVERYDAY COOKING by Patti Ballard. The newest and freshest in our famous wine cookbook series. Patti is the popular wine consultant from Santa Cruz who has been impressing winery visitors and guests for years with her wine recipes and the cooking tips from Patti's grandmother. Chapters range from soup and hors d'oeuvres through pasta, fish and desserts—all of course using wine. 128 pp, illustrated, 8½″ x 11″, ppb, $5.95 @ ISBN 0-932664-20-2, Oct. 1981.

#721 CALIFORNIA BRANDY DRINKS, "The One Bottle Bar" by Malcolm R. Hébert. Cocktails, coolers, punches, holiday nogs, coffee and tea drinks, ice cream and dessert drinks. Over 500 recipes from "The Angel's Kiss" to the "Zoom". Also, short history, tasting quide, cooking and mixology tips. Suitable for the brandy enthusiast or professional bartender. 160 pp, $4.95 @ ISBN 0-932664-21-0.

HOW TO ORDER BY MAIL: *Indicate the number of copies and titles you wish on the order form below and include your check, money order, or Mastercard, or VISA card number. California residents include 6% sales tax. There is a $1.50 shipping and handling charge per order, regardless of how many books you order. (If no order form—any paper will do.) Orders shipped promptly via U.S. Mail—U.S. & Canada shipments ONLY. Telephone orders welcome. Call toll-free 800-231-WINE or (415) 566 3532.*

ORDER FORM
THE WINE APPRECIATION GUILD
1377 Ninth Avenue
San Francisco, California 94122

SHIP TO: _____

Address _____

City _____ State _____ Zip _____

Please send the following:

_____ Copies #500 EPICUREAN RECIPES OF CALIFORNIA WINEMAKERS	$6.95@	_____
_____ Copies #501 GOURMET WINE COOKING THE EASY WAY	$5.95@	_____
_____ Copies #502 NEW ADVENTURES IN WINE COOKERY	$6.95@	_____
_____ Copies #503 FAVORITE RECIPES OF CALIFORNIA WINEMAKERS	$5.95@	_____
_____ Copies #504 DINNER MENUS WITH WINE	$6.95@	_____
_____ Copies #505 EASY RECIPES OF CALIFORNIA WINEMAKERS	$6.95@	_____
_____ Copies #527 IN CELEBRATION OF WINE & LIFE	$25.00@	_____
_____ Copies #554 WINE CELLAR RECORD BOOK	$32.50@	_____
_____ Copies #640 THE CHAMPAGNE COOKBOOK	$6.95@	_____
_____ Copies #641 POCKET ENCYCLOPEDIA OF CALIFORNIA WINES	$4.95@	_____
_____ Copies #671 CORKSCREWS "KEYS TO HIDDEN PLEASURES"	$20.00@	_____
_____ Copies #672 CALIFORNIA WINE DRINK BOOK	$4.95@	_____
_____ Copies #673 WINE IN EVERYDAY COOKING	$5.95@	_____
_____ Copies #721 CALIFORNIA BRANDY DRINKS	$4.95@	_____
_____ Copies #727 WINE LOVERS' COOKBOOK	$6.95@	_____
_____ Copies #734 THE ODYSSEY COOKBOOK	$8.95@	_____
_____ Copies #860 CALIFORNIA BRANDY CUISINE	$6.95@	_____

California Residents 6% sales tax _____
plus $1.50 Shipping and handling (per order) $1.50
TOTAL enclosed or charged to credit card _____

Please charge to my Mastercard or Visa card # _____

Expiration Date _____

Signature _____

The Wine Appreciation Guild Books
"The Classic Series on Cooking With Wine"

This series of ten wine cookbooks is the largest collection of cooking with wine recipes available in the World. There is no duplication of features or recipes in the Wine Advisory Board Cookbooks. Specific wine types are recommended as table beverages for all main dishes. The present series represents over 3,000 different recipes of all types using wine. From wine cocktails, hors d'oeuvres, salads, soups, wild game, fish, eggs, many different main dishes to desserts and jellies; the magnitude of this collection of wine recipes is overwhelming. Who could possibly develop and test such a large number of recipes? These books are the result of the cooperation of over 400 people in the wine industry. In 1961 the Wine Advisory Board

began collecting the favorite and best recipes of various winemakers and their families. Most of the recipes are old family favorites, tested with time and then re-tested and proven in Wine Advisory Board test kitchens. We are particularly pleased with the recipes and wine choices from staff members of the Department of Viticulture and Enology and the Department of Food Science and Technology of University of California, Davis and Fresno.

So here is a series of the very best wine recipes; selected and developed by many of the most knowledgeable wine and food lovers of America.

#500 EPICUREAN RECIPES OF CALIFORNIA WINE-MAKERS: Did you know that you can buy wild boar, cook it at home with Burgundy and produce a gourmet treat that your guests will rave about for years? Or, that you can make your reputation as an Epicurean cook by preparing and serving Boeuf a la Bourguinonne, according to the recipe of a famous wine authority? This book includes the most elaborate to simple recipes contributed by California Winemakers, their wives and associates; all selected for their unforgettable taste experiences. Another important feature of this book is the comprehensive index of recipes for the entire six cookbook series, 128 pp, 8½" x 11", illustrated, 1984 edition. $6.95 @ ISBN 0-932664-00-8.

#501 GOURMET WINE COOKING THE EASY WAY: All new recipes for memorable eating, prepared quickly and simply with wine. Most of the recipes specify convenience foods which can be delightfully flavored with wine, enabling the busy homemaker to set a gourmet table for family and friends with a minimum of time in the kitchen. More than 500 tested and proven recipes; used frequently by the first families of America's wine industry. 128 pp, 8½" x 11", illustrated, 1980 edition. $5.95 @ ISBN 0-932664-01-6.

#502 NEW ADVENTURES IN WINE COOKERY BY CALIFORNIA WINEMAKERS: New Revised 1984 Edition, includes many new recipes from California's new winemakers. The life work of the winemaker is to guide nature in the development of wine of beauty, aroma, bouquet and subtle flavors. Wine is part of their daily diet, leading to more flavorful dishes, comfortable living, merriment and goodfellowship. These recipes contributed by Winemakers, their families and colleagues represent this spirit of flavorful good living. A best selling cookbook with 500 exciting recipes including barbecue, wine drinks, salads and sauces. 128 pp, illustrated, 8½" x 11", $6.95 @ ISBN 0-932664-10-5.

#503 FAVORITE RECIPES OF CALIFORNIA WINE-MAKERS: The original winemakers' cookbook and a bestseller for fifteen years. Over 200 dedicated winemakers, their wives and colleagues have shared with us their love of cooking. They are the authors of this book, which is dedicated to a simple truth known for thousands of years in countless countries: good food is even better with wine. Over 500 authentic recipes, many used for generations, are included in this "cookbook classic". Revised Edition 1981. 128 pp, 8½" x 11", illustrated, $5.95 @ ISBN 0-932664-03-2.

#504 DINNER MENUS WITH WINE By Emily Chase and Wine Advisory Board. Over 100 complete dinner menus with recommended complimentary wines. This book will make your dinner planning easy and the results impressive to your family and most sophisticated guests. Emily Chase worked with the winemakers of California a number of years and was also

the Home Economics Editor of Sunset Magazine. She tested recipes for six years and is the author of numerous articles and books on cooking. This edition contains 400 different recipes, suggestions for wines to accompany dinners and tips on serving, storing and enjoying wine. 1981 Edition, 128 pp, illustrated, 8½" x 11", $6.95 @ ISBN 0-932664-30-X.

#505 EASY RECIPES OF CALIFORNIA WINE-MAKERS: "I wonder often what vintners buy one-half so precious as the stuff they sell" questioned Omar Khayyam 1100 A.D. We wonder what the vintners could possibly eat one-half so delicious as the food they prepare. This is a collection of "precious" recipes that are easy to prepare and each includes the vintner's favorite beverage. Many are recipes concocted in the vintner's kitchens and some are family favorites proven for their flavor and ease of preparation. No duplication with the other cookbooks. 128 pp, illustrated, 8½" x 11", $6.95 @ ISBN 0-932664-05-9.

#527 IN CELEBRATION OF WINE AND LIFE: "The Fascinating Story of Wine and Civilization" by Richard Lamb & Ernest Mittelberger. With art reproductions from The Wine Museum of San Francisco. The origins, customs and traditions of winemaking and wine drinking explored in depth and explained through the art work and lore of wine through the ages. Such important subjects as wine and health and love are covered as well as the hows and whys of selecting, cellaring and appreciating wine. 35 Full Color plates and many rare prints richly illustrate this intriguing book. Revised 1984 Edition, 248 pp, hardbound, 10" x 8", $25.00 @ ISBN 0-932664-13-X.

#554 WINE CELLAR RECORD BOOK: A professionally planned, elegant, leatherette bound cellar book for the serious wine collector. Organized by the wine regions of the World, helpful for keeping perpetual inventories and monitoring the aging of each wine in your cellar. Enough space for over 200 cases of wine and space to record tasting notes and special events. Illustrated, 12" x 10½", six ring binder, additional pages available. $32.00 @ ISBN 0-932664-06-7.

#640 THE CHAMPAGNE COOKBOOK: "Add Some Sparkle to Your Cooking and Your Life" by Malcolm R. Hébert. Cooking with Champagne is a glamorous yet easy way to liven up your cuisine. The recipes range from soup, salads, hors d'oeuvres, fish, fowl, red meat, vegetables and of course desserts—all using Champagne. Many new entertaining ideas with Champagne cocktails, drinks and Champagne lore are included along with simple rules on cooking with and serving Sparkling Wines. Recipes are provided by California, New York and European Champagne makers and their families. The author's 30 years of teaching and writing about food and wine makes this an elegant yet practical book. 128 pp, illustrated, 8½" x 11", ppb, $6.95 @ ISBN 0-932664-07-5.